CLIMBERS THREE

Dennis Wynne-Jones

Fisher King Publishing

Climbers Three

ISBN 978-1-910406-28-1

Published by
Fisher King Publishing
The Studio
Arthington Lane
Pool-in-Wharfedale
LS21 1JZ
England

Contents

ACKNOWLEDGEMENTS

The writing of this book would not have been possible without the help and generosity of so many people. My thanks to the staff of the West Yorkshire Archive Service in Leeds and Bradford, and to the staff of Ilkley Library. Also thanks to Mike Gibbons, the Reverend Michael Savage and the staff of Kendal Archives.

There was valuable assistance from Peter Lucas of the Fell and Rock Climbing Club, who arranged the loan of Blanche Eden-Smith's Diaries; and also from Maxine Willett, Archivist at the Mountain Heritage Trust in Penrith, who gave access to Harry Kelly's Diaries and who took a great interest in the idea of the book. Margaret Clennett, Archivist of the Pinnacle Club, was a tremendous help and support throughout the research period.

A big thank you to the Fell and Rock Climbing Club and the Pinnacle Club for permission to quote from their Journals, and to the Pinnacle Club for permission to reproduce some of their photographs.

The title of the book comes from a poem in 'Mountain Lure' by George Basterfield. The poem is called 'Memories' and seems a perfect description of a typical mountain day for our three sisters from breakfast to bed.

Finally, thank you to my long-suffering wife Tricia, who spent many hours listening without complaint while I rambled on about Trilby Wells and her sisters.

Dennis Wynne-Jones

INTRODUCTION

When a short obituary appeared in the Ilkley gazette on the second of August,1985, readers were informed of the death of a local lady, Emily Wells, at the age of 96.There was a brief reference to her many mountaineering exploits and a few hints about other aspects of her life.

Having met and interviewed Miss Wells, as she preferred to be called, I began to uncover a life of variety, adventure, dedication and innovation. She was a 'founder' in every sense of the word, and a pioneer of new methods of educating children with special needs.

Emily Wells and her two rock-climbing, mountaineering sisters were born in the small hamlet of Denton, near Ilkley in West Yorkshire, but moved at an early age to Ben Rhydding. Soon the three sisters acquired nicknames: Annie became 'Paddy', Emily became 'Trilby', and younger sister Sarah Ellen (sometimes known as 'Nellie') became 'Biddy'.

There were links in the lives of the three sisters to the Church of St. John at Ben Rhydding; to the local ladies Hockey Club; to the founding of the first ladies-only mountaineering club in Britain; to Bradford Diocesan Council meetings; to the Munros of Scotland; to the Margaret Macmillan methods of education; to many leading and famous mountaineers of the day; to local operatic and Gilbert and Sullivan societies; and to some incredible 'firsts' in the world of mountaineering.

A shy, modest lady in her later years, Trilby Wells insisted in her interviews that nothing be written about her and her sisters during her lifetime. In respect of her wishes, my notes have remained on file for many years, but now I hope I can illustrate the varied and active lives of the three sisters with some justification. This story hopefully will be of interest not only to local people in Ilkley and Wharfedale, but also to students of mountaineering history nationally and internationally.

CHILDHOOD AND THE DENTON CONNECTION

Between the years of 1835 and 1852, ten children were born to farmers Hannah and Thomas Wharton, living at Denton, a small hamlet near Ilkley on the north side of the river Wharfe in West Yorkshire, England. The last two children were twins, Jane and Sarah, both baptized in the local church of St. Helen on May 2nd, 1852. As the family grew older and the children left home, Jane, who was in domestic service, returned home to look after her widowed mother when her father Thomas died on June 12th, 1876. Little is known of what happened to Jane's nine siblings, but Jane Wharton was herself to have six children, all born in Denton, after she married Cooper Wells in Denton church in 1882. Three of her six children were to form the major part of this story.

Denton at that time was a rural, agricultural hamlet, most of the surrounding land being owned by the family living at Denton Hall. The Hall estate dates back to 1253, being owned at one time by the Fairfax family, before being sold about 1700 to Henry Ibbetson of Leeds. The Ibbetson family developed the estate, especially the farming side, and became well known as breeders of shorthorn cattle. Sir John Ibbetson commissioned Robert Carr of York, an associate of the great architect Robert Adam,to build Denton Hall as we see it today. The work was completed in 1778 by Carr (who also designed Harewood House, near Leeds) and cost one hundred thousand pounds.

The estate passed through marriage to the Wyvill family in 1845, and it is here that Cooper Wells enters the story. Cooper, named after his mother's maiden name, was a stonemason living in Hunton Parish, near Bedale in North Yorkshire. Marmaduke Darcy Wyvill lived at Constable Burton Hall in Wensleydale and married Isabella Price, who bore him a son also called Darcy. By marriage to Laura Ibbetson, daughter and heiress of Sir Charles Ibbetson,Bart. of Denton Park, the Wyvill family became the owners of the Denton estate. Darcy needed someone to help run the estate land at Denton so appointed Cooper Wells to the post. Born in 1848, Cooper had followed his father into the trade of stonemason and had lived in Wensleydale all his life, but moved to lodgings in Denton to begin his new job. Next door to his new home in Denton lived a young lady called Jane Wharton, with her widowed mother Hannah. There were lots of Whartons mentioned in Parish reords of the time, and it was a popular name in the hamlet. Romance obviously blossomed, as Cooper and Jane met regularly, attended local functions and sang together in the church choir. Suffice to say they were duly married on September 27th 1882 at Denton church. Three other daughters of Thomas and Hannah Wharton, sisters of Jane, were also married in the same church- Martha in1870, Margaret in 1871 and Sarah in 1875. Jane and Cooper's six children would all be baptized in the church of St. Helen between 1884 and 1895, and oldest daughter Annie (Paddy) was married to John Hirst, mountaineer and poet, at Denton in1922. The church of St. Helen certainly had a strong connection with the Wells family. As an aside, it was noted about this time that no record existed for the date for the official Dedication of the church, so on June 19th, 1890, the church was formally Dedicated to St. Helen by the Right Reverend the Lord Bishop of Ripon, H. Boyd Carpenter D.D., assisted by the vicar R.Bullock M.A. and other local vicars. A collection was made of £11-6s-3d (£11.31p) and donated to Ilkley Hospital. Most of the Wells family were present at this Dedication.

The vicar, Rev. Bullock, was the man who baptized all the Wells children. Annie was the first born, being baptized on June 15th 1884; sister Mary was born in 1886 and brother Thomas in 1887. Two years later, on 3rd July, Emily was born and was baptized on August 11th 1889. John followed in 1891, and then there was a gap of four years before youngest child Sarah Ellen was born on March 22nd and was baptized on May 5th 1895. The family of Jane and Cooper Wells was now complete. Annie, Emily and Sarah Ellen were to become the leading characters in this story.

Denton Church.

Shortly, the whole family would move across the river to Ben Rhydding as their home in Denton was too small for a family of eight, but not before Hannah Wharton, grandmother to the children, passed away in 1888. Hannah, her husband Thomas and brother-in-law Samuel were all buried in the same grave in the small churchyard at Denton. Later, Cooper and Jane Wells, daughter Mary (who died aged 34), and son Thomas were also buried in the churchyard of the church of St. Helen.

So into the world came the three sisters who were destined to be involved in mountaineering history in future years. Their childhood was rural, pastoral and family orientated, and Trilby (Emily) spoke of the affection and camaraderie between the family members. She enjoyed her childhood, being at first educated at home by her father Cooper. By 1901, when Trilby was twelve, the family were in their new home in Ben Rhydding, to the east of Ilkley. The address was Westmead, 19 Moorland View, an address that no longer exists. Painstaking research has gone into locating Moorland View, as it only existed up to the 1940's.

Turning off the A65 into Ben Rhydding opposite the metal bridge over the Wharfe, there are two terraces of Victorian houses (now separated by a short row of more modern homes) on the left hand side of Wheatley Lane. The higher of these two terraces was known as Moorland View, built facing west towards Ilkley and backing onto farmland towards the east. It was to here that the Wells family moved. Near the top of Wheatley Lane is a footpath leading to Hangingstones Road and eventually to the Cow and Calf Rocks, which Trilby recalled using with her sisters on their way to and from the Moor and the Rocks.

By 1901, Emily/Trilby had passed an examination at the age of eleven for acceptance into Salts Girls High School where she worked exceptionally hard and was apparently a model pupil. Later, younger sister Biddy/Sarah Ellen also attended Salts school. They travelled daily by train to Saltaire and Trilby again describe her school days as enjoyable, even suggesting that it was this enjoyment that gave her the idea of becoming a teacher herself. Once again, her younger sister followed suit and also took up teaching. In fact, older sister Annie/Paddy had set the precedent as she was the first of the three sisters to qualify as a teacher. In the 1901 census Annie is described as a "Pupil Teacher-School", aged 16, and in the 1911 census she is described as a 26 year-old "School Teacher". Incidentally, the 1901 census lists their mother Jane as 49 years old, but then describes her as head of the household. There is a mention of her husband Cooper Wells in the 1901 census though he is simply described as "male, stonemason, aged 53". However, all the family were still living at Moorland View in 1901 and in 1911, but Thomas Wells was later to move to Bradford, becoming a grocer.

By 1905, at the age of sixteen, Emily Wells left school and began her training as a teacher, working at a school in Ben Rhydding. Later, in 1918, she would transfer to a school in Bradford, the Margaret Macmillan School, catering for children with special needs. Her contribution to education in Bradford, and her innovative ideas are described later.

As teenagers (though the term was not in use in those days), the three sisters had become active in several sports, playing hockey and tennis at school, and enjoying walks to local beauty spots such as the Cow and Calf Rocks, Rombalds Moor, Otley Chevin and the Addingham/Bolton Abbey area. In one of her later interviews, Trilby spoke of the long walks that she and sister Biddy took, being out all day, especially in the summer months. During the years up to the Great War, they spent many weekends enjoying the local countryside. Older sister Annie, meanwhile, often ventured further afield, and on her visits became fascinated by the sight of people rock climbing, particularly in the Lake District. Most rock climbing and mountaineering at the time, before 1918, was very much a male preserve, but there were a few keen ladies pushing their way into a male dominated sport. Annie Wells was very keen to try her hand at rock climbing and in 1916 she met Harry Kelly and his party, including his wife Emily, while they were climbing at Laddow Rocks on the Pennines. Annie was hooked, and completed several climbs that day with Harry Kelly. Incidentally, Mrs. Kelly, though named Emily, was usually called Pat. However, when a mountaineering club hut was later named after her it was called the Emily Kelly Hut. Pat Kelly was to become a close but short-lived friend of all three Wells sisters.

It was at this time that Annie acquired the nickname of "Paddy", which was to stay with her for the rest of her life. She had met the Kellys at Easter of 1916 and both she and Pat Kelly encouraged more and more women to join the outdoor meets. It was Pat Kelly who gave Annie the nickname of Paddy on a climb at Laddow, though sister Trilby could not remember why this name was chosen. She thought it might have been because Annie 'padded' up the climbs in her rubber soled shoes! Neither could Trilby remember in her interviews how she and Biddy acquired their nicknames. However, the year 1916 became a turning point in the life of Paddy Wells and consequently for her two sisters.

N.B. For the sake of clarity, the names Paddy, Trilby and Biddy will be used for the rest of this story.

LOCAL PRECEDENTS

It was not surprising that people from this area should be interested in exploring and enjoying the countryside- it was all around them. The forbidding hulk of Rombalds Moor overlooked their homes, and the crags of Ilkley and Almscliff were nearby. People journeyed all over the moors of the area for generations, usually with a purpose- i.e. travelling from Wharfedale to Airedale, or tending to animals on the moors. But later, they began to walk for walking's sake, particularly in the Victorian era, when people realised the benefits of the open air, and the enjoyment of being closer to nature.

Rocky Valley, Ilkley.

As early as 1787, the vicar of Otley, the Rev. James Bailey, had been a keen walker, and on an excursion to Scotland, had ascended Ben Nevis. Accompanied by a Lieutenant Walker, who was stationed at Fort William, Bailey joined a group of eleven men, with three local guides, who left at 6.00 a.m. from Fort William. A Mr. Kayne was the second civilian in the group, and the provisions for the journey were carried by two sergeants and three privates of the Royal Fusiliers. After seven hours, the arduous ascent was achieved; there was no proper path nor track up the mountain and in places a rope and grappling hook were used. On reaching the summit, the party celebrated with food and alcoholic drink, before 'trundling boulders' over the cliffs! This seems utterly incomprehensible today, but in 1787 Ben Nevis would hardly have been busy; and this practice seemed to be quite popular amongst mountaineers at the time. After a short time on the summit, the party descended, taking six more hours to reach Fort William. The Rev. Bailey of Otley had completed one of the earliest ascents of Ben Nevis, and was possibly Wharfedale's first 'mountaineer'.

Very little other local evidence of walking and climbing exists until we come to the Victorian period. People began exploring their local area and then travelled further afield. The Lake District and Snowdonia, and also the Pennines, became popular areas for long and short holidays but most of those who visited these areas were of a certain social class. Only those who could afford to visit- in terms of time and money- could travel such long distances. There are, however, records of people from Horsforth, Ilkley, Skipton and Shipley, Bingley and Keighley, visiting the Lake District in the 1860's and 1870's, and many more from the cities of Leeds and Bradford. They were of course mainly professional people such as JohnJudson,a Keighley Draper; Cornelius Clarke, Owen Owen and Adam Smith of Skipton; William Exley and Thomas Armstrong of Shipley; and the Laycock brothers of Keighley. These men – in those days mountaineering was mainly a male preserve- visited Langdale and Wasdale in the Lakes, climbing mountains and scrambling up and down steep gullies. They were part of the early Lakeland pioneers.

There were also visits to North Wales, with climbs on Lliwedd, near Snowdon, and on Tryfan in the Ogwen valley. All three Wells sisters were to climb in Wasdale and on Tryfan on numerous occasions, Trilby being there when a tragic accident happened.

Two more famous local characters also explored the local moors, dales and crags before venturing onto far bolder exploits in the mountains of the Lake District. William Cecil Slingsby of Carleton, near Skipton, and Geoffrey Hastings of Silsden, were frequent visitors to the climbing centres of Wasdale, Coniston and Langdale in the 1870's and 1880's, often accompanied by their respective brothers, John Arthur Slingsby and Cuthbert Hastings. All were mountaineers and rock climbers, and put up several new climbs in the Lake District. Cecil Slingsby in particular was well respected in mountaineering circles and was a founder member of the Fell and Rock Climbing Club of the English Lake District (often referred to as the FRCC).Although the Wells sisters didn't know him personally they were great friends with his daughter, Eleanor, who was later to marry the mountaineer Geoffrey Winthrop Young.

In his thirties, Slingsby was very fit and strong, and had started climbing in Norway in 1872. He became an expert on Norway and the Norwegian people took to him; he became almost a legend in Norway, even in his own lifetime. He made the first ascent of Store Skagostolstind, one of the highest of Norway's peaks, on his own, after his companions turned back. He explored mountains and glaciers, wrote a book on Norway, learnt the local language, studied Scandinavian legends and became interested in the flora and fauna of Norway. His book 'Norway: the Northern Playground' was warmly received both in Britain and in Norway and is still a collector's item today.

William Cecil Slingsby.

Cecil also climbed in the Alps, particularly on the Chamonix Aiguilles, including the first ascent of the Dent du Requin in 1893 with close friend Geoffrey Hastings, Mummery and Collie. He climbed in the Lake District with Hastings, W.P. Haskett–Smith (author of the first ever climbing guide in the British Isles), and with the Hopkinson brothers, O.G.Jones and Godfrey Solly, all famous names in the annals of mountaineering history. Skye, Ben Nevis and other parts of Scotland were also visited, and he was also an explorer of potholes and caves in the Yorkshire dales. He became Pr esident of several mountaineering clubs in his time and was an active member of every club he joined.

But he never forgot his roots. He loved his home village of Carleton, where he lived at Beech House and where his family owned the local mill. He was involved in the church choir, played the organ, organized concerts in the village and was perceived by everyone to be a happy and friendly man. He loved to walk at Malham and in the area of the Yorkshire Three Peaks, as well as on Rombalds Moor. Many locals were to follow his pioneering spirit.

Thus, towards the beginning of the twentieth century, mountaineering as a sport had become more popular. More people were visiting the mountains of Britain as well as journeying further afield to the Alps, Norway and even to the Himalayas. In the Fell and Rock Club's list of members, there are many names from the Bradford, Keighley and Skipton areas listed in the first years of the club. Mountaineering clubs were being formed in several areas of the country, including the Climbers Club in 1888, but this was mainly for professional, moneyed people. The Alpine Club in London had of course been going since 1857 and had helped to inspire many people to explore mountains abroad. In 1892, Cecil Slingsby became the first President of the newly-formed Yorkshire Ramblers club; and in 1902 the Rucksack Club (men only and based in Manchester) was started, followed by another men-only club from Liverpool, the

Wayfarers Club, in 1906. That same year saw the formation of the Fell and Rock, based in the Lake District, which welcomed both men and women into membership. This was significant, and related very much to our three sisters from Ben Rhydding, as all three later became FRCC members, and all three were instrumental in setting up a ladies-only club after World War One.

Initially the FRCC comprised mainly Lakeland climbers, but it soon became evident just how popular the club had become as members joined from all over the U.K. Local members include W.S.Tetley of Wheatley Lodge, Ben Rhydding; J.F.Seaman of Kirkfield, Ben Rhydding; J.J.Brigg of Kildwick Hall near Keighley;and of course the Slingsby and Hastings brothers. In the Yorkshire Ramblers early Ilkley and Ben Rhydding members included J.S.Crawford, R.M.Mather and J.N.Longfield, plus several others from Wharfedale. In later interviews, Trilby Wells said they knew of many local residents who were active in climbing circles in the early part of the twentieth century, but could remember no particular names.

The Ladies Alpine Club was set up in 1907, but it was to be 1921 before a ladies-only climbing club was established. This of course was the Pinnacle Club, and all three Wells sisters were involved in the club from the start. There is however some evidence that, prior to this, they were already involved in a club in Ilkley, as it is thought that Trilby and Biddy Wells were members of an Ilkley Rambling Club in 1919 and 1920. The story of the founding of the Pinnacle Club follows later.

So the idea of walking and climbing locally as well as in the mountains of Britain and Europe was quite a familiar concept in the Ben Rhydding and Ilkley area, and it is no surprise that the three sisters became proficient mountaineers. What is so amazing is how they found the time to climb and walk in the Dales, Lakes, Wales, Scotland and the Alps whilst leading such busy lives.

Several locals had indeed taken up rock climbing as a pastime and although people had scrambled on local outcrops for many years, roped climbing was beginning to grow in popularity. Climbing had started at Almscliff Crag, near Otley, in the early1890's, with pioneers such as Fred Botterill and Walter Parsons. An early guidebook to Almscliff appeared in 1913 and inspired both locals and climbers from further afield to explore the crag. C.D.Frankland, between 1910 and 1920, put up several new climbs, and another guidebook appeared in 1923. In her interviews, Trilby Wells mentioned these guidebooks, and talked of travelling by train to Weeton station and walking up to Almscliff for their 'training'afternoons on the crag.

Ilkley, too, boasted an interesting crag, though not until the 1930's was there a route at the now popular Cow and Calf Quarry. Climbers were drawn to an area slightly further south of the Cow and Calf, to crags known as 'Rocky Valley', where the Yorkshire Ramblers members had been exploring since about 1911. There were also interesting crags on top of Simon's Seat, near Bolton Abbey, and at Rylstone and Crookrise, both near Skipton.

Further away, a very popular crag was Laddow, on the Pennines, accessible by road or rail from Manchester, Barnsley or Sheffield. A one hour walk from road or station led to a series of climbs on a gritstone outcrop, and it was for this crag that the Rucksack Club members produced a guide to the climbs in their 1911 Journal. Laddow became well-known to all three Wells sisters and it was here that Paddy first met the Kellys. Climbing had started here in 1903/4 and towards the end of World War One, Harry Kelly greatly increased the number of routes. As stated previously, the Kellys became great friends of the Wells family, and Pat Kelly initiated the founding of the Pinnacle Club. Laddow was also the venue for one of the first meetings of Paddy Wells and John Hirst, who were to marry in 1922. Harry Kelly attended their wedding but unfortunately, Pat Kelly had been killed in an accident in 1921. The story of that tragic day is told later.

MOUNTAINEERING LADIES IN THE 19th AND 20th CENTURIES

Prior to the Wells sisters taking up mountaineering, the sport had mainly been male dominated. There were however lots of female pioneers in the late nineteenth and early twentieth centuries, particularly from Britain. Sometimes accompanied by their husbands, and often using local guides, women had been climbing and exploring in the Alps for many decades, though there were examples of women-only expeditions as early as 1874. In the book 'Swiss Notes by Five Ladies', there is an interesting account of five ladies, three of them from Yorkshire, travelling by train, then by horse and carriage, to Chamonix, Zermatt, Lugano and Pontresina. They walked and climbed in several areas, and three of them (Grace Hirst of Halifax, Fanny Richardson of Doncaster and Minnie Neilson of Scotland) were the first all-female group to climb Mont Blanc. The other Yorkshire lady was Mary Taylor of Gomersal, who acted as a kind of chaperone and was known on the journey as 'Frau Mutter'; she later became an author, climbed in New Zealand and the Alps and was a friend of the Bronte sisters, having attended school with Charlotte Bronte. The sister of Fanny Richardson, Katherine, was an early member of the Ladies Alpine Club, moving to live in the Alps and who completed over one hundred ascents (including Monte Rosa and the Matterhorn), many of them first ascents. Here was a prime example of exploration, tenacity, bravery and not a little skill by Yorkshire women.

One of the first English women to climb in the Alps was the well-known Lucy Walker who made the first female ascent of the

ALMESCLIFF CRAG. (101)
A singular and very conspicuous knob of gritstone rock, 700 ft. above the sea and 1½ miles from Weeton Station. From its isolated position, the cliff commands a fine all-round view of the valley of the Wharf.
Almescliff Crag

Almscliff Crag, today and in 1922.

Matterhorn in 1871. Other women followed, including Amelia Edwards, E.P.Jackson and Mary Mummery; they were all noted not only for their climbing prowess but also for the fact that they wrote about their exploits as well. Elizabeth Le Blond also climbed in Norway and the Alps and wrote several books about her expeditions.

These books helped to increase awareness amongst men and women of the skill and courage shown by women climbers from Great Britain.

In the second half of the nineteenth century women received little support for, and often opposition to, their climbing. There was little acknowledgement in society in general of climbing as an activity for women. The Alpine Club (men only) had been formed in 1857 but the Ladies Alpine Club would not come into existence for another fifty years. Some women returned from their Alpine exploits and talked of the criticism, unfriendliness and even hostility towards their adventures from men both at home and abroad. In fairness though, there was already a small minority of men who positively encouraged women to climb, and this continued until the Wells sisters were climbing in the 1920's.

By 1900, when the Wells family were in the process of moving to Ben Rhydding, more men accepted women as climbers, and the development of the 'cordee feminine'- women climbing 'sans homme'- was a concept accepted by many more men. Women had generally climbed in skirts and boots up to that time, but more and more of them now wore knickerbockers or breeches. Boots were still heavy and nailed, and women would often walk to crags in a skirt and boots, removing the skirt at the crag to reveal the 'bockers' underneath when well away from prying eyes. As late as 1913 someone wrote that "a woman in knickerbockers was an object of derision or shame!"

However, climb they did, and in 1904 Mrs. Le Blond gave an interesting lecture to the Yorkshire Ramblers on her exploits at home and abroad. This lecture is quite a milestone in the history of the acceptance of women as mountaineers, as it signified recognition by one of the leading clubs of the era.

In 1906 the Fell and Rock Climbing Club of the English Lake District (what a grand title and surely the best-named club in Britain) was formed welcoming both male and female climbers. An earlier chapter mentions the links between early Wharfedale and Airedale residents and this famous club, and in 1907 there appeared an article in the club Journal entitled "A Ladies Week at Wasdale". The article praised the abilities of the ladies present, particularly Annie and Evelyn, daughters of George Seatree (club Vice President), and lists ten days of climbs completed by the ladies, including the probable first female ascent of Eagles Nest Arete. Also listed were Kern Knotts Chimney, Scawfell Pinnacle, Gable Needle and climbs on Pillar, and it was noticeable that two of our local Yorkshiremen, Slingsby and Hastings, were involved in leading some of the ladies on these routes. Many of these climbs were later ascended by the three Wells sisters.

Climbing was also developing in the mountains of Wales around the same time, and in 1906 several climbs were put up on the cliffs of Lliwedd, the Milestone Buttress, Glyder Fach and the Idwal Slabs. Women climbed on many of these routes up to the start of the Great War including Mrs. Orton (Rowan Route in 1910) and Miss E.M. Barlow (Cneifion Arete in 1905, Pulpit Route in 1911 and various routes on Tryfan). On Lliwedd Mrs.Farmer put up Central Gully in 1906 with the famous Oscar Eckenstein and A.W.Andrews. Other female pioneers in North Wales included Edith Stopford on Lliwedd, Ann Bridge, Katherine Hopkinson, Mabel Northcote and Ruth Mallory. Eleanor Slingsby of Carleton, Skipton, with her brother Laurence, led routes on Tryfan before 1914 and was a frequent visitor to Snowdonia.

At Easter 1907, a tradition of holding an annual climbing meet at

Pen-y-Pass, near Snowdon, was begun by Geoffrey Winthrop Young, whose record of Alpine ascents and exploration was well known; so too were his climbs in Wales, the Lakes, Scotland and Ireland. Many leading mountaineers, and later their families, attended these meets, including several female climbers, and the meets were equally famous for their social gatherings in the evenings after a hard day on the crags. These social evenings were to be continued later at early Pinnacle Club Meets attended by the Wells sisters. Professional people, particularly from Oxford and Cambridge Universities, teachers from public schools, professors and leading mountaineers attended at Young's invitation, and many new routes resulted. Young positively encouraged the female members of the party to climb as well, and in 1921 he was to provide tremendous encouragement to the ladies who set up the Pinnacle Club. Young was also to marry Eleanor ("Len"), daughter of Cecil Slingsby, towards the end of the Great War; Len became a great friend of all three Wells sisters.

Scotland, too, had become a venue for women climbers with Mrs. Inglis Clark (benefactor of the C.I.C. Hut on Ben Nevis) climbing the first summer ascent of South Castle Gully on the Ben in 1911. She had already climbed the first winter ascent of Central Trident Buttress in 1904 with her husband and another famous Scots mountaineer Harold Raeburn. Other first ascents she completed in 1901, 1902 and 1903. George Abraham's wife (from Keswick, Cumbria) also completed first ascents on Buachaille Etive Mor in October 1900, and a certain Miss B. Jones was climbing first ascents on Skye in 1911.

Thus the years before the Great War saw a great increase in women climbing, locally, nationally and internationally. Then in 1911 a mountaineering event occurred which is closely linked to our three Wells sisters, particularly Trilby and Biddy. On June 11th of that year, two members of the Fell and Rock Club, Messrs. Leslie G. Shadbolt and A. McLaren, completed the first traverse of the main Cuillin Ridge on the Isle of Skye. The various peaks had all been climbed individually, or in small groups, much earlier, but the traverse of the whole ridge from end to end had so far eluded everyone. It was to be 1928 before the complete ridge was traversed by an all-female party for the first time. That party included Trilby and Biddy Wells from Ben Rhydding, and is described in a later chapter. In 1911, the two men left Glen Brittle at 3:35 a.m., taking just less than seventeen hours to complete the traverse. In the 1911 Fell and Rock Journal, Ashley P. Abraham wrote: "I feel sure that June 10th, 1911 witnessed one of the most remarkable feats of endurance, and mountaineering and climbing skill, ever accomplished in our home mountains". This puts into perspective the later achievement of Trilby and Biddy Wells in 1928.

Another event connected to the Wells family (Paddy this time) had occurred twenty years previously, when in 1891, in the Scottish Mountaineering Club Journal, Sir Hugh Munro produced the first list of Scottish mountains over three thousand feet (914.4m.) high. Known thereafter simply as Munros, to date over four thousand people have completed the ascent of all these peaks. Munro listed 538 summits, of which 282 were seen as 'separate' summits. This list is significant in our story as Paddy Wells/Hirst and her husband John Hirst became the ninth and tenth people ever to complete the list of ascents in 1947.

John Hirst, later to marry Paddy after the death of his first wife, had been Head Boy at Oundle School and then studied at Trinity College, Cambridge. He helped to found the Manchester electrical engineering company of Hirst, Ibbetson and Taylor after his studies and was an active mountaineer from a very young age. Before the

Great War he had climbed extensively in the U.K. and in the Alps, and was an early member and generous benefactor of the Rucksack Club. There is more about John Hirst in a later chapter.

1911 had also seen the death of a well-known alpinist and mountaineer, Edward Whymper, and in 1912 J.M. Archer-Thompson, headmaster climber and guide-book writer, had tragically committed suicide.

Meanwhile, Paddy, the oldest of the three Wells sisters, was beginning her mountaineering career. She attended a holiday in the Lake District organised by the Holiday fellowship, where she met a lady climber. Already a keen walker on the hills, Paddy was keen to try climbing and they both completed several routes together, though it is not known where exactly they climbed. This lady turned out to be Lilian Bray, the daughter of Lord Justice Bray, and she was a future member and founder of the Pinnacle Club. Known as an excellent leader of climbs and a strong mountaineer who still walked the Snowdonia hills in her seventies, Lillian Bray was to accompany Trilby and Biddy Wells on their traverse of the Cuillins on Skye in 1928. With Paddy Wells and Dorothy Pilley-Richards, another famous climber, she also climbed guideless in the Alps and in the Dolomites. She walked the Pyrenees and the Tatra mountains, and served in France as a hospital masseuse in World War One. She was also a talented actor, joining Trilby and Biddy in one-act plays or sketches at club meets; she particularly loved the Yorkshire meets of the Pinnacle Club, and became a lifelong friend of the Wells sisters, sometimes staying at their home in Ben Rhydding. The initial chance meeting of Lilian and Paddy in the Lakes led to a future in climbing and mountaineering for all three of the Wells sisters. As Paddy's progress in climbing developed, so she came under the influence of H.M. Kelly and his colleagues, who were some of the leading climbers of the day. In due course, Trilby and Biddy (still known as Emily and Nellie) were to meet up with this same group of climbers, and began scrambling, then roped climbing, at places such as Almscliff Crag, Widdop, Laddow and later in the Lake District.

Sadly, 1914 was looming and with it came the threat of a major war. Climbing was still increasing in popularity and numerous new routes were put up in England, Wales and Scotland. Perhaps the greatest feat of 1914 was the first ascent of Central Buttress on Scafell, by Herford, Samson and Holland, another milestone in climbing history, especially as it demanded a new grade of climb be created. The route was graded Very Severe (hard) and remained the hardest climb in the Lake District for two decades.

On a personal note, at the turn of the century, the Wells sisters had embarked on their teaching careers. Paddy had obtained a Board of Education Certificate and then taken further examinations, obtaining parts one and two of the Higher Certificate of the National Froebel Union. In 1905 she obtained her first teaching post. Trilby and Biddy also obtained Board of Education Certificates and both passed the Joint Board of Northern Universities Metriculation Exams. In 1909, Trilby started her first teaching post, followed by Biddy in 1913. All three sisters had trained as pupil-teachers in local schools, before becoming certificated teachers, and were placed on the new Teachers Registration Council lists in 1920. Both Trilby and Biddy were soon to move to the Margaret Macmillan School at Thackley, near Bradford, while Paddy taught in the Lancashire and Cheshire area.

Back in Wharfedale, climbers were still active at Almscliff Crag and Rocky Valley as well as many climbers making the journey up to the Lake District or across to North Wales. With the improvement in transport, even Scotland was visited by local climbers, particularly at Easter, Whitsun and Summer Bank Holidays. Paddy Wells, now aged about twenty, continued to visit the Lakes and stayed at Wasdale on a few occasions before 1914. She became aware of the increase in women mountaineers, but also how popular with women the sport of rock climbing was becoming. Trilby, at fifteen, and Biddy, about nine, could only look on enviously, and Trilby in her interviews spoke of the vicarious joy they had when Paddy returned home to tell her younger sisters about her latest exploits.The seed was sewn in Trilby and Biddy.

THE GREAT WAR YEARS

The years 1914-18 were of course the Great War years, but they were also important in Paddy Wells' development as a rock climber and mountaineer. Fortunately, two people kept diaries of their climbing exploits during this period, and again fortunately, both of these diarists were companions of Paddy Wells and occasionally her two sisters. One diarist, H.M. Kelly, known to most people as H.M.K., or simply Kelly, was a leading rock climber of the period. He lived in Levenshulme, Manchester, and journeyed out to the hills and moors of the Pennines on a regular basis, almost every weekend of the year. There is a great deal of mystery about Kelly, in that no-one really knew what he did for a living. He worked from a small office in Fountain Street, Manchester, during the week, and when war broke out in 1914 he remained in England, not being called up nor volunteering for active service. Nor was he known as a Conscientious Objector. Nor is it known if he had any health problems which prevented active service. For example, it was known that George Abraham, with varicose veins, and Ashley Abraham, with T.B., were excused war service, but Kelly appears to have been fit and healthy.

Suffice to say, Kelly remained very active on more peaceful activities during the war years, and his early diaries contain references to climbing at Laddow and Almscliff, and visiting Ben Rhydding and Ilkley where he no doubt stayed with the Wells sisters. As was the practice in the early part of the twentieth century, Kelly would climb up and down routes, often with his wife following or leading, on both gritstone outcrops on the Pennines and also on Lake District crags. In 1916 his diary records twenty-six routes in a day, ascended and descended, and this after travelling for several hours to the crag. He could afford to run a car during and after the war years, but we do not know how he made his money. He could even afford to travel to the Alps, to Norway and even as far as Russia for his mountaineering and exploring. He was a man of immense character and great technical skill on rock; the Wells sisters were to learn a lot from H.M. Kelly and his wife Pat.

The other diarist was Blanche Eden-Smith, an early member of the FRCC and later a founder member of the Pinnacle Club. She began her diaries in 1916 and was to climb with all three Wells sisters in future years. She also spent many years as a climbing partner of H.M. Kelly, particularly after the death of Harry Kelly's wife Pat in 1922. Mrs. Eden-Smith also inherited a nickname, that of Gabriel (after the angel Gabriel) and this was later shortened to G. There are several references in Kelly's later diaries in which she is simply listed as G; the name was given to her soon after the setting up of the Pinnacle Club in 1921. We should add here that Blanche had started her climbing career by following her husband up climbs, and later turned to leading routes. She and her husband were regular visitors to Wasdale, Coniston and Borrowdale during the early years of the war, and G was a regular partner to each of the Wells sisters after the war.

A further mention needs to be made concerning the names of people in this period of social history. In many records of climbs and walks, men and women are often listed simply by letters-e.g. H.M.K. or G.W.Y.; at times they are simply called by their surnames-e.g. Kelly, Beetham or Cain; in other records they are much more politely called by their titles and surnames, particularly the women climbers-e.g. Miss Wells, Mrs. Kelly or Dr. Corbett.

So in the Great War years, Paddy Wells was becoming active in the leading climbing circles. We know that she had visited the Lake District in about 1910 with a Holiday Fellowship group, and a repeat visit was made at the start of the war. Paddy climbed once more with Lilian Bray, and becoming great friends, the pair decided that a trip to the Alps would be the next step for them in their advancement in climbing skills. Trilby later said that there was no shortage of advice from experienced male alpinists when the two women suggested this trip, though several stressed the importance of using local guides. So the trip to the Alps finally materialised, and it was on this visit that Paddy made the acquaintance of several English climbers, one of whom was John Hirst of Manchester. He encouraged the ladies to lead climbs and also to climb without male companions; he must have developed a great admiration for Paddy Wells as he was eventually to marry her in 1922.

So when Paddy, already a climber in 1916, met the Kellys, she extended her climbing experiences and her abilities. Whilst Kelly was known to have a stubborn and tough personality, he could also be sincere and friendly to those he liked. He loved music, singing and cricket, and again encouraged the evening 'sessions' of music and drama after a day's climbing. Although his favourite crag was Pillar, he completed many first ascents on other Lake District crags, such as Kern Knotts, Tophet Bastion, Moss Ghyll Grooves and on Scafell. He was a very early guide-book writer too, along with C.F. Holland, George Bower and George Basterfield, and as a later editor he completely changed the format of the new series of the Lake District guides. He visited Laddow and other Pennine outcrops on a regular basis, climbed on Tryfan and Lliwedd in Wales, and also visited Ben Nevis and Skye with J.H.B. Bell, another mountain pioneer and writer. Indeed, it is suggested that it was Kelly who had introduced 'rubbers' (rubber soled tennis shoes- often from

Woolworths!) to climbing whilst on the Cioch on Skye in 1915. However, Kelly had already used rubbers in the Lakes, as had other contemporary climbers, but it did set a trend which others followed.

So, for the three Wells sisters to climb with a man of such vast experience was a real boost to their development as climbers. Much of their early climbing was on gritstone, which was hard, and also rough on the hands. Trilby again spoke of this in her later interviews, and said what a good experience it gave them before venturing onto bigger crags in the Lakes and Wales.

Meanwhile, in the year that Paddy had started climbing with the Kellys, the 1916 Fell and Rock Journal published an interesting article by Mrs. H.M. Waterlow entitled "Climbing for Women". At a time when many women were doing men's jobs (during the war years) the article suggested that old conventions still lingered and that to some people climbing was not an activity for women; and this was reflected in many of the 'men-only' climbing clubs around the country. Mrs. Waterlow's article makes fascinating reading, and she finished by suggesting that it is better for a woman to lead an easy climb than to be led up a harder climb by a man! Women were indeed becoming more prominent in climbing adventures and this was to increase considerably after the war.

At the same time, other famous female mountaineers were 'learning the ropes'. Dorothy Pilley (later Mrs. Richards) did her first roped climb in 1915 with Herbert Carr, and then continued to climb throughout the war years. She was later to go on to many great ascents in several parts of the world. Eleanor Slingsby, too, was also climbing, as were Blanche Eden-Smith and Pat Kelly. So too the likes of Florence Ormiston-Chant; Emily Hilda Daniell (who put up Hope on the Idwal slabs and who also used the pseudonym E.H.Young as a novelist); Ilse Bell (sister of J.H.B.Bell); Ruth Mallory; Nea Morin;

and Mabel Barker. Most of these women were to become members of the Pinnacle Club and were friends and associates of the Wells sisters.

The last named of these, Mabel Barker, was a person of great interest to the Wells sisters, particularly Trilby and Biddy, not only for her climbing abilities and experiences, but also for her pioneering and innovative ideas for education. Born at Silloth, Cumbria, in 1885, Mabel barker trained at Cheltenham Ladies College before gaining a B.Sc. from London University in1907. She loved the outdoors and was a keen botanist from an early age. Before the Great War she had completed lots of walks among the Lakeland fells and undertook a walking tour of the Scottish Highlands in 1910. She met a Lake District 'character' called Millican Dalton, an accomplished climber and early member of the Fell and Rock, and climbed with him up to the start of the war.

During the war years, Mabel Barker worked in Edinburgh until 1915, before travelling to Holland in April 1916 in order to help Dutch and Belgian refugees, returning to England in 1917. Mabel had studied the educational ideas of people such as Froebel, Dewey, Montessori, Charlotte Mason and Margaret Macmillan during her formative years, and now realised the great potential of a 'new' kind of education. It would be 'experiential' education in every sense: out of doors, interdisciplinary, with practical work, exploration and skills learning (very much an early form of 'adventure education'?) combined with some classroom-based activities. She hoped in this way to develop a more rounded individual, a 'freer' child, able to express opinions and be at home in the local outdoor environment, almost at one with nature. She did at some time meet Geoffrey Winthrop Young (at one time a school inspector) and he was a sympathetic ear to these ideas and ideals; Young felt that education in

Britain's schools was too 'narrow'. Mabel also met George Mallory, a supporter of Young's ideas on education, seeing the need to introduce a balance between practical outdoor tasks and experiences, and work in the classroom.

This is relevant to Trilby and Biddy Wells as they introduced many new ideas into the Margaret Macmillan School in Bradford in later years. During her later interviews, Trilby Wells was asked about who she had met, visited, climbed with, talked to, dined with, etc. Apart from naming some very famous mountaineers, it transpired that both Trilby and Biddy had actually visited Mabel Barker's school in Cumbria after it was set up in 1927.

On Mabel's return to England, she had worked at Kings Langley Priory School in Southern England, where progressive education was the norm. The local environment had to be included in the curriculum, and apart from the more academic lessons, there were sessions of gardening, animal keeping, flower and vegetable growing, outdoor games and exploration, art, pottery and embroidery. Interestingly, there was also an emphasis on personal and health care, one of the many ideas the Wells sisters later introduced into their school in Bradford. No doubt the meetings between Mabel barker and Trilby and Biddy Wells, both at Mabel's school and on the mountains, were very fruitful.

By 1916, Paddy Wells was 32 years old and climbing regularly. Trilby, then 27, later said that she and 21 year old Biddy would listen intently to Paddy's tales of days spent climbing, and on her regular trips home she would accompany her younger sisters up to the local crags at Ilkley. There she would discuss routes and techniques with them, and also took them to Almscliff Crag in lower Wharfedale as part of their 'climbing education'. The Wells sisters were now embarked on a lifelong love of the mountains.

However, in December 1916 Paddy furthered her mountain experience in a way she would never forget. On Friday December 22nd, Paddy was staying at Stove End in Langdale with H.M.Kelly and two others, probably the Eden-Smiths. They decided to attempt Central Gully on Great End, and took three hours to reach the bottom of the gully in snowy conditions. There they stopped to eat their lunch. Once embarked on the climb they were often knee-deep or even waist-deep in soft snow in the bottom half of the gully and were nearly smothered in a minor avalanche. As conditions seemed better higher up they continued, until in the top half of the gully the party was hit by a second and final avalanche. The leader (Kelly) had called out a warning, but the entire party were swept of their feet and tumbled down the gully. They were fortunate that there was so much snow that it covered the rocks completely, and they fell two hundred feet in about ten seconds. They came to a stop partially buried, but with heads above the snow level, breathing hard. Paddy sustained a bruised thigh, Kelly a twisted knee, the others uninjured. After recovering Kelly's lost ice axe, they made their way back to Esk Hause in a blizzard, before descending Rossett Ghyll in waist-deep snow and then on down to Mickleden. After a change of clothes and a hot meal, Kelly recorded in his diary that they could laugh about the experience! However, Kelly stayed in bed for the next few days still troubled by his twisted knee, though Paddy on December 27th was well enough to climb Pavey Ark and the Langdale Pikes. It would appear that Kelly, Paddy and the others were very fortunate not to finish 1916 with serious or even fatal injuries.

In a journal of the Fell and Rock Club, there are two anonymous articles, describing quite vividly the events of this avalanche; they are very similar to the entries in the diaries, and are well worth a read. It is thought that the articles were written by Kelly and Blanche

Eden-Smith (but anonymously to avoid embarrassment), as they were both members of the FRCC at the time. Paddy Wells did not become a member of the club until 1918.

1917 dawned and Biddy Wells began to join Paddy and the Kellys on some of their climbs. At Easter of that year the party were climbing at Wharncliffe and at Laddow, where dozens of routes were climbed. Some were led by Kelly with Paddy following, others with Biddy following. On Saturday April 7th Kelly and Biddy completed a remarkable sixteen climbs of moderate or difficult standard, plus several routes with Paddy also on the rope. Interestingly, in Kelly's diaries, he calls Paddy "Miss Wells" but her sister is called by her nickname of Biddy. It was also an important day for Biddy as she led several of the routes, under Kelly's guidance, including Scylla and Pillar Staircase at Laddow, seconded by Paddy and with Kelly third on the rope.

Two of the Wells sisters continued to climb through that summer, but two important events also occurred in the summer of 1917. In August, Laurence Slingsby, son of Cecil and brother of Eleanor, was tragically killed on active service. He had been an active climber pre-war, having climbed with Geoffrey and Len Winthrop-Young. Then on September 7th, Young himself, after suffering horrendous injuries, had his leg amputated in Italy. This was a devastating blow to Young, and most climbers might have felt that meant an end to their mountaineering career. Not so Geoffrey Winthrop-Young! After the war, he learnt to walk and climb and repeated many routes in North Wales, even returning to the Alps to climb again.

That month, September 1917, again saw Paddy in the Lakes with Kelly, climbing on Great Gable on the 7th. They climbed Arrowhead Arete Direct, Eagles Nest Arete, Abbey Buttress and Eagles Nest Ordinary Route. In December, Paddy was back again, climbing Middlefell Buttress in Langdale on the 23rd, and the next day climbing Great Gully, Pavey Ark, and Gwynne's Chimney. The next day was spent walking from Langdale to Easedale Tarn with the Kellys. Paddy had had another exciting year.

Trilby and Biddy Wells continued to walk and climb in their home area, and also took up more seriously their other interests of playing tennis in summer and hockey in the winter. It is interesting to note that both sisters were instrumental in setting up the ladies hockey team which later became part of the Ben Rhydding Sports Club. The men's team was formed in the 1922-23 season and in the history of the club there is praise for "Miss Wells" (Trilby) for her great support and who was honorary secretary in the opening season. Trilby spoke much later of her involvement in the founding of the ladies' team before the men's team, on a Radio Leeds programme broadcast in 1980, called 'Meet the Folks' with John Ancombe. She said that she and Biddy had started the hockey club in 1921, playing women-only teams at first, then later mixed teams. She also said she played "right inside, then right half, then right back"! However, there is evidence of ladies teams playing unofficial matches on fields in the Ben Rhydding area immediately after the Great War, and visiting Leeds, York and Wakefield. This unofficial team may have begun after friendly matches were held between ex-Ilkley Grammar School girls and ex- Otley Prince Henry's Grammar School girls during and after the war. Trilby mentioned these games in her interviews (though she and Biddy had never attended the Ilkley school) and talked about how much she and Biddy had enjoyed playing hockey and tennis before the 1920's.

Trilby and Biddy also devoted time to their other great love in the years of the war. She and Biddy had become regular worshippers at the Church of St. John in Ben Rhydding, barely half a mile from their home. Trilby, again in her radio broadcast, spoke about her long association with the church, where she was a Sunday School teacher for a while, a Church Council member and a devoted organiser of social events for fellow church members. Later she was to become a representative of the church at the Diocesan Council in Bradford, and records show her attending meetings and conferences for the next forty years. Once again there is a link to her mountaineering days, as Trilby used to love to organise dramatic and comedy sketches, plays, singalongs,etc. for the church groups, just as she did in the evenings at Pinnacle Club meets after a hard day on the crags. She was ably assisted by Biddy in all these dramatic ventures, writing scripts together, composing poems and ditties often related to local people and events. One Parish Church newsletter reports how "the Misses Wells brought the house down with their topical sketch and the screaming play which they produced entitled 'Acid Drops' with which the evening closed". And when Sunday School Festivals were held, Biddy and Trilby not only managed the productions, they wrote the sketches and even made some of the costumes. Other notable one-act plays were called 'Bloaters', Behind the Bathroom Door' and 'Shocks in a Parish!'- all apparently hilarious, well performed and well received. The Wells sisters also organised quizzes, games, handicrafts, any questions, whist drives, talks and tennis groups. One activity which was a favourite with church members was a "Quiz-Ramble" around the local area, again organised by the sisters.

Both sisters were working full time as teachers and they were to work together for many years at a special school in Bradford. It is hard to appreciate the energy and effort they both put into their lives, combining teaching by day; social and dramatic events by night; hockey and tennis games; church meetings and conferences; yet still active as climbers and walkers. In addition, they were extremely generous towards the church, providing prizes for events and fund raising regularly. Of course there was just enough time for one more activity for Trilby- her love of music. She was an avid fan of Gilbert and Sullivan, and she sang with the Menston Amateur Operatic Society for twenty years. Rehearsals were held in Menston prior to the performances in Ilkley. From there, Trilby later joined the Bradford Gilbert and Sullivan Society, and remained a patron up to her death in 1985. So how Trilby and Biddy still found time to visit Ilkley crags and Almscliff Crag, plus occasional trips to the Dales and the Lake District, is quite astounding.

So to 1918 and Paddy Wells continued to climb regularly. That year Paddy joined the Fell and Rock Club, as did Dorothy Pilley. Here Paddy was to meet and mix with most of the top rock climbers of the day. There were at that time really two main 'schools' of climbers- the FRCC, who tended to spend most of their time in the Lake District, and The Climbers Club (CC), London based but who mainly climbed in North Wales. Both these great clubs are associated with the development of climbing in these two areas, and there was some overlap in their choice of climbing venues. The result was a tremendous advance in standards of rock climbing and an increase in the creation of new climbs in the early part of the twentieth century. The FRCC welcomed women climbers into membership and this was a great boost to the development of female climbing in the U.K.

Blanche Eden-Smith records her adventures in the Lake District in 1918, including climbing on Scafell, Great End and Great Gable. H.M. Kelly too was active in these areas in the early part of 1918, as well as climbing with Paddy Wells at Laddow in April. A rainy day stopped them climbing in the morning, but a drier afternoon meant Paddy could climb three routes with Kelly. Incidentally, Kelly also wrote articles for the Rucksack Club Journal, and in 1918 produced a piece called 'Laddow-New Photographs and New Climbs'. There were several other occasions in 1918 where Paddy climbed with Kelly and his wife, both on gritstone and Lakeland crags, but there was one personal event in 1918 which sadly affected all three Wells sisters.

On September 5th, 1918, Cooper Wells, father of the sisters, sadly passed away aged seventy, and he was buried in the tiny churchyard of Denton, across the river Wharfe from the family home in Ben Rhydding. The gravestone records his death; and three other family members who died later are also recorded on the gravestone- Jane, his wife, Mary, his daughter and Thomas, his son. Cooper Wells' grave thus continued the link that the Wharton and Wells families had established with the beautiful little church of St. Helen in Denton. By coincidence, the man who had first employed Cooper Wells to work at Denton Hall Estate, Darcy Wyvill, also passed away later that same month, on September 23rd,1918.

In the autumn of 1918 all three Wells sisters were again active. Trilby, however, tended to be more of a walker and scrambler than a climber, and it was Biddy and Paddy who continued the family trait of rock climbing and mountaineering. Other women were also putting up new climbs, including Dorothy Pilley, who made the first ascent of Original Route, Holly Tree Wall at Idwal, Snowdonia in May 1918. Also, H. R.C. Carr had led no less than five ladies up a new route on Dow Crag 'E' Buttress in August. Women were now leading climbs more frequently and standards were rising.

Then in November 1918 came the Armistice and the end of the Great War. In her book "Women on High", Rebecca A. Brown suggests that "World War 1 marked a social and cultural watershed... women emerged with a new sense of freedom and opportunity... Mountaineering remained an unusual sport, but it started attracting more and more people outside the ranks of the very wealthy." More women were certainly taking to climbing as a sport, and were more willing to climb in women only groups. They also wanted first ascents! In her interviews, Trilby Wells talked of climbing with men in the post-war years. "We met a lot of male climbers, some famous ones; some were a bit down on us, but lots of them were very encouraging". She particularly mentioned Kelly and John Hirst, and said that she climbed with other local men at Almscliff Crag, Otley Chevin, Embsay and Ilkley. When Trilby later climbed in the Lake District, she described the men, mainly FRCC members, as "always supportive", encouraging the ladies to climb and to lead.

Paddy was by now an active member of the FRCC. The Kellys now lived at Cheadle Heath, Manchester and the Eden –Smiths at Grange over Sands, so the Lakes was an ideal venue to meet and climb. Cecil Slingsby had now left Carleton and moved to Milnthorpe, and Silsden mountaineer Geoffrey Hastings was now in Bradford. However they were all united in their membership of the Fell and Rock. John Hirst, however, though extremely active in Lake District climbing, did not join the Fell and Rock until 1920.

The three Wells sisters were by now mixing with members of several clubs, notably the Yorkshire Ramblers, Wayfarers, Rucksack Club, the FRCC and the Climbers Club, as well as several members of the Alpine Club. This enabled Paddy and Biddy in particular to increase their experience, knowledge and climbing techniques. The post- war years were beckoning and the opportunities to further advance their mountaineering careers.

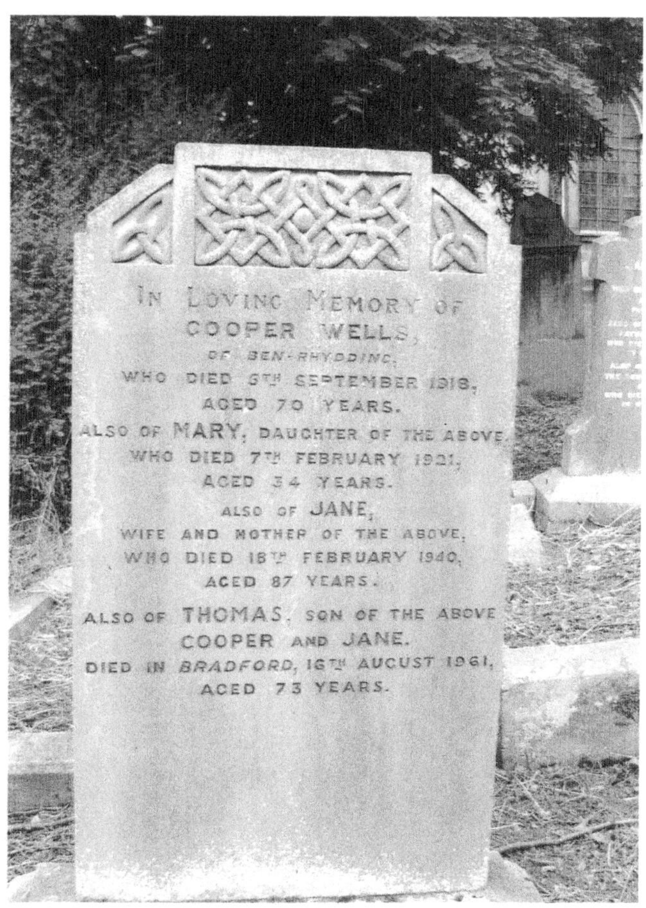

Wells family grave, Denton Churchyard.

THE POST-WAR YEARS

November 1918 was a memorable occasion for the country as a whole, and Blanche Eden-Smith and Beatrice Thomas, to celebrate the Armistice, placed a Union Flag on the cairn on top of Scafell Pike. H.M. Kelly and Paddy Wells climbed in the Lakes late that year and when 1919 began they were again in the Lakes.

In spring 1919 Kelly spent some time in Derbyshire, with John Hirst and Paddy among the group. Paddy had met John a few years before, both in the Alps and on gritstone crags. Meanwhile Biddy climbed on her local Wharfedale outcrops, and introduced Trilby to several of the routes at Almscliff, where they were occasionally joined by Paddy when she returned home for a weekend. Trilby could remember the names of routes in her nineties, including Fluted Columns, Cup and Saucer and some chimneys, as well as referring to climbing all over Low Man. Her description of their 'gear' was enlightening- hemp rope, hemp waistline or direct tie on the waist (with a bowline), woolly hat (Almscliff is always windy!) and nailed boots with tricounis. She described their progression to 'gym shoes', and said how excellent they were on gritstone in dry weather, but "no good at all in the wet!" The climbs at Almscliff were accessed by walking uphill from Weeton station, close to the Harrogate-Bradford road, or on occasions walking from Otley station, via Leathley and Stainburn. In later years, the Pinnacle Club were to hold meets at Almscliff Crag and sometimes hired a cottage at nearby Castley, close to Pool-in-Wharfedale.

Trilby's climbing education continued, being taken up to the crags above her home and also to the Rocky Valley outcrops. Trilby mentioned how hard the climbs seemed at Ilkley and that most of the time she simply scrambled over the boulders. She did some climbing however, though felt that was not enough to entitle her to become a 'full' founder member of the Pinnacle Club in 1921. It was to be a few years before most of the routes at Ilkley were first climbed, and Ilkley Quarry, nowadays so popular, was not really developed until the 1930's. The Yorkshire Ramblers members had also begun exploring the chimney lines at Rylstone and Crookrise Crags near Skipton, often led by W. Cecil Slingsby.

Mabel Barker, meanwhile, had been climbing with Millican Dalton in the Lake District in winter during the war years, and had joined his camping trips to Epping Forest in the summer. In 1919 she was again n the Lakes with Dalton. Also in 1919, Geoffrey Winthrop Young, despite his handicap of losing a leg in 1917, was putting up new climbs with Len on Lliwedd in Snowdonia. Len was now Mrs. Winthrop-Young, having finally agreed to marry Geoffrey in 1918. She had first met Geoffrey at her home in Carlton near Skipton in 1903 when he visited her father Cecil Slingsby- she was seven years old- and he had taken her and her brother Laurence climbing in 1911 when she was fifteen and Laurence seventeen. Geoffrey had apparently proposed to Len in 1914 but at eighteen she was not agreeable to this. After his injury and amputation, he returned home and proposed again in January 1918. Suddenly, by April he was a married man; Geoffrey was forty-one, Len was twenty years younger. Geoffrey's brother Hilton was injured in a wartime raid and unable to attend as best man, but the ceremony went ahead on April 25th 1918, with the Slingsby and Young families and many famous mountaineers in attendance. Cecil Slingsby gave his daughter away. They soon started a family, son Jocelin being born in 1919 and daughter Marcia in 1925.

Also by 1919, the newly weds were climbing regularly in Wales. So too were Dorothy Pilley and Pat Kelly, who were by now also putting up new routes in Wales. H.M. Kelly was also very active in the Lake District, holidaying there for three weeks, culminating in the ascent of Tophet Bastion, a superb and difficult route. His wife Pat was holidaying and climbing with him, but it is interesting to note there is little reference to the ascent or to his wife in his diaries. Later in 1919, there was a FRCC meet at Torver, Coniston, and Paddy Wells was in attendance. To give an example of the company that Paddy was keeping at the time, also on the meet were such famous climbers as Raeburn and Solly, as well as Dorothy Pilley. Paddy climbed on Doe (sic) Crags all weekend.

Middle Row Cottage, Wasdale.

Biddy and Trilby Wells were also involved in a rambling club in Ilkley at the time, and Trilby said that when she first joined the Pinnacle Club she had listed her experience as more of a rambler than a climber. Thus she did not become a full member of the Pinnacle Club, just an 'associate member, until 1925. There are references to the rambling club in local newspaper reports of the time.

Sadly, in 1919, Sir Hugh Munro, who had listed the Scottish mountains in his Munros tables, passed away. He had produced the list in 1891, and this list was to inspire Paddy Wells to accompany her husband John in completing the ascent of all these peaks.

The year finished with H.M. Kelly, John Hirst and Paddy Wells attending a Rucksack Club meet at Laddow, followed by a club dinner. They were back on the crags at Kinder in January 1920, before planning an Easter meet in North Wales. There, Paddy climbed Hope, on the Idwal slabs with Kelly on Tuesday April 6th, before descending the Ordinary Route. More weekend meets followed throughout April and May at Laddow with John Hirst and Kelly, before a Whitsun meet at Wasdale, where Paddy was joined by sister Biddy. The meet, led by Kelly, saw a large group gathered at Middle Row at Wasdale Head. On the first day, in brilliant weather, Biddy climbed Kern Knotts West Buttress, while Paddy did West Chimney, also on Kern Knotts.

Paddy Wells, who was a full member of the Fell and Rock, was really getting into her stride, and the end of July saw her spending the bank holiday weekend at Pen-y-Gwryd in Snowdonia, again with Hirst and Kelly. Paddy climbed Pinnacle Route on Lliwedd with both men, and her partnership with John Hirst was beginning to blossom.

Not to be outdone, Trilby was by now climbing occasionally on Almscliff Crag, and also playing hockey. On Friday January 20th 1920, the local Ilkley Gazette reported that the Ben Rhydding Ladies Hockey Team had beaten Harrogate 6-5 and had previously beaten Sandal 7-2. Trilby remembered playing several matches at various venues in Yorkshire along with sister Biddy. Trilby and Biddy were living in Ben Rhydding at this time and were also heavily involved in the local church social groups.

Also, Kelly's wife Pat was leading harder and harder climbs, including first ascents She had married Kelly before the Great War, and they had climbed together continuously for several years. Many thought of Pat as being as good a climber as her husband on certain routes, and both of them often soloed climbs (i.e. with no ropes) together, sometimes both up and down routes. There were no children to the marriage and thus they were able to climb or walk almost every weekend and holiday. They had a car, quite a luxury in 1920, and had the money, time and transport to travel to the Pennines, the Lakes, Wales and Scotland on a regular basis. It was the Kellys who introduced the Wells sisters to Middle Row in Wasdale, where they were to spend many happy days in the future.

Middle Row is a cottage situated just a few yards from the hotel at Wasdale Head. Now part of the nearby farm, the two-storey cottage has been used by climbers and walkers since the beginning of the twentieth century (if not before then) as a perfect base for their activities in the western parts of the Lake District. Footpaths from Middle Row lead in all directions; up to Sty Head and thence to Borrowdale, Langdale, the Gables and the Scafell range;and to Mosedale and then on to Pillar. It was a long journey by road to the head of Wasdale in the 1900's, and some early mountaineers even accessed Middle Row by travelling by train to Windermere station and continuing by carriage to Langdale, before walking over Sty Head Pass and down the long path to Wasdale Head. All this prior to exploring the crags or fells of the area before repeating the journey in reverse. They were certainly fit and tough!

Autumn 1920 saw Paddy and John Hirst climbing at Windgather

in September and at Laddow in October. On October 24th Paddy took Biddy to Laddow to climb with Hirst, and in November all three were again in the Lakes attending the FRCC meet at Coniston. Paddy also attended the 1920 annual Fell and Rock Dinner, at which there were one hundred and sixteen members and guests. It is not known if her two sisters were part of the guest list.

On a professional note, in the summer of 1920 all teachers had to be placed on a list held by the Teachers' Registration Council, and on August 1st of that year Paddy Wells (registered as Annie), teacher number 46557, was duly registered. Her professional address was given as 'Grivola, Boarden Lane, Marple, Cheshire, where she was later to live with John Hirst. On September 1st 1920, both Trilby (number 53840) and Biddy (number 54481) were registered, and by this time both were teaching at the Margaret Macmillan School in Bradford.

Thus 1920 finished on a high note for the Wells sisters. They were part of the growing influence of women in the climbing scene. Pat Kelly had suggested several years before that it would be a good idea to have a climbing club exclusively for women. Nea Morin, in her book 'A Woman's Reach', suggests there was still some prejudice towards women in climbing circles after the war. However, lots of women were in agreement with Pat Kelly, and men like Young, Hirst and several prominent members of the Fell and Rock positively encouraged the idea. Young in particular suggested they held a meeting to explore the idea and Pat Kelly and Len Young agreed. Women leading climbs was still quite a rare sight, even with a man as second on the rope. All-women ropes were even more rare, but Pat and Len were keen to encourage women climbing together.

Trilby Wells, reflecting in her interviews in the 1980's, said that "we had determination and a lot of spirit in those early days….yes, we followed the men, we copied them, asked them questions and took advice; but we really enjoyed climbing together as women… a bit of showing off really" with a chuckle and a smile. Trilby also said that when she became a climber, the women often climbed short single pitches on the longer Lakeland routes, the men tending to string together several short pitches into one long pitch. She added: "we often climbed routes in a different way and a different style to the men". I think she was also referring to the fact that many women were not as physically strong as men and so needed to use more balance, poise and grace; and though sometimes slower on a route, they spent more time working out moves, whereas men often simply used their upper body strength to overcome certain moves. This is not to belittle the women climbers of this period, as many of them were extremely fit and indeed very strong both physically and in character.

So 1921 began and it was to be a momentous year in the history of women's climbing, not just with the formation of the Pinnacle Club. Various women put up new routes in the Lake District and there were now female members on the FRCC committee. For the Wells sisters, Laddow was again the first venue of the year, on January 8th, when Paddy and Biddy again climbed with Hirst and Kelly. Blanche Eden-Smith was winter climbing on Dow Crag in February and was to be found on Idwal slabs in March, climbing the Ordinary Route and Charity in torrential rain.

Bad news for Paddy and her sisters arrived in February, however, when their younger sister Mary, who had been suffering from a severe bout of flu, passed away.

Paddy had to return home to Ben Rhydding to be with her sisters Trilby and Biddy, her brothers Thomas and John, and her mother Jane. The funeral was held the following week at the Church of

St. Helen, Denton, and Mary was buried in the same grave as her father. Trilby later spoke only briefly about her sister Mary, saying that Mary was quite different to the other three sisters, lacking the adventurous spirit and energy of the three mountaineers. Trilby also said that John Hirst attended the funeral, accompanying Paddy as a friend. This was an omen for the future as the following year they were to marry in the same church.

Away from this personal loss for the three sisters, things were moving fast in the world of women's mountaineering. The idea of an all-female club had gathered momentum and its formation was imminent.

THE PINNACLE CLUB AND EARLY 1920s

1921 saw the formation of the Pinnacle Club, the first all-female mountaineering club in England at the time. This was momentous not only for all female climbers and mountaineers, but also for the three Wells sisters who became Founder Members of this great club. There is plenty of literature written about the origins and founding of the Club, and I can recommend reading Shirley Angell's excellent 1988 book on the Pinnacle Club, and its history of women climbing.

In 1921 there were more and more women taking to the mountains, both as climbers and walkers. Many parties were by now all-female, and the Wells sisters were part of this change. Trilby Wells was 32 years old and teaching in Bradford, alongside her 26 year old sister Biddy. They continued to ramble, scramble and climb locally, Biddy also climbing further afield. They also joined sister Paddy on several occasions in 1921 to either walk or climb together. The idea of an all-women climbing club had been discussed so often that an inaugural meeting was planned. One of the prime movers, probably THE prime mover, was Emily (Pat) Kelly, who wrote a letter to the Manchester Guardian, announcing to the public that the inaugural meeting was to take place at Easter 1921 in North Wales. This letter was duly published, accompanied by a short leader by the editor, Mr. C.E. Montague, praising and supporting the idea of a female club, suggesting that it was inevitable that such a club would be formed and that the present time was the right time. This support was added to by Geoffrey Winthrop Young and Harry Kelly. It was suggested that Eleanor (Len) Winthrop Young be President, and an agenda and proposed rules were drawn up.

THE PINNACLE CLUB.
WOMEN'S ROCK CLIMBING CLUB. 41
++++++++++++++++++++

Application for Membership Form. 1921

Date March 26th

Name. (Mrs.or Miss) Trilby Wells....

Address...19..Moorland View........

.........Ben Rhydding...

State whether the application is for Full or Associate Membership. ......Associate......

Particulars:-

(If possible, state year when mountaineering and climbs done).-

Mountaineering in N. Wales and Lake District – also on Pennines.

Trilby Wells application form for Associate Membership, the Pinnacle Club, 1921.

And so, on March 26th, 1921, the Inaugural Meeting of the Pinnacle Club took place in the billiard room of the Pen-y-Gwryd Hotel, in the heart of Snowdonia. Before the meeting several of the ladies had spent the day climbing or walking. Blanche Eden-Smith was on the Milestone Buttress of Tryfan, and recorded her exploits (and the later meeting) in her diaries. Len Winthrop Young had been on Snowdon that day, while Pat Kelly had climbed with Paddy Wells on Tryfan. In order to become a Full Member of the Pinnacle Club, applicants had to prove that they could lead a climb of moderate difficulty; others who couldn't achieve this could become Associate Members. Paddy and Biddy Wells thus became Full Members, while Trilby applied for Associate Membership, as she was not regularly leading climbs at that time.

The club also had the object of fostering the independent development of rock climbing amongst women, and all members had to subscribe to this objective. It is interesting that some application forms contained lists of climbs 'descended' as well as 'ascended', a familiar practice in climbing circles in the 1920s.A total of forty three ladies signed up as aspiring original members, fourteen of whom were FRCC members. Here was another source of support for the ladies, as the Lake District Club enthusiastically welcomed the formation of the Pinnacle Club. So too did the Rucksack Club of Manchester. A few of the original Pinnacle members soon fell by the wayside for various reasons, but most remained loyal to the club. Len Winthrop Young, for example, was still a member until her death in 1994 at the age of ninety eight. In 1921, John Hirst composed a song about the founding of the Pinnacle Club, and the 1921 FRCC Journal published a three-page article about the Pinnacle Club by "Mrs. Kelly", expressing thanks for the help and support of "our big brother" the FRCC. The list of Original Members of the Pinnacle Club included Lilian Bray, Florence Ormiston-Chant, Lella Michaelson (Blanche's sister) and Dorothy Pilley (later Mrs. Richards), as well of course as the Wells sisters. Twenty Full Members were accepted and twenty three Associate Members. Pat Kelly was elected Secretary, Blanche Eden-Smith as Recording Secretary and Paddy

Wells as a committee member. It is worth noting that Len Winthrop Young, the new President, described Blanche as the "Recording Angel", so called her Gabriel. This quickly became her nickname, later shortened to "G"; and this is how she is often referred to in the future diaries of H.M. Kelly, with whom she regularly climbed after 1922. She also climbed with all three Wells sisters in the 1920s.

The first official climbing meet of the Pinnacle Club was held on the following day, on Tryfan, a favourite venue with so many of the members. It is ironic that Pat Kelly led the meet on Tryfan, the venue for her tragic death a year later.

So the Wells sisters played their part in the setting up of the Pinnacle Club. Paddy Wells was to become the club's second President; Trilby, too, was later to become President; and Biddy was a committee member for many years.

1921 continued as an active year for the three sisters. Paddy and Biddy, and eleven other Pinnacle members, joined a Fell and Rock meet at Gimmer Crag, Langdale in April. The two of them also climbed with Harry Kelly and friends at Laddow in April, and in the summer a Pinnacle Club Lakeland Meet was held at Torver, near Coniston. This time, Biddy was joined by Trilby, both of them climbing with Pat Kelly from July 30th to August 3rd. They climbed mainly on Dow Crag, in "lots of rain" according to Kelly's diaries, but got lots of routes done. Biddy also completed two routes on Dow with Blanche Eden-Smith. This was a great few days for Trilby Wells in particular, as the experience she gained in climbing on Dow enabled her to improve her climbing techniques and skills. She was the least experienced of the three sisters at that time. On 4th August, Trilby was climbing again, on High Neb at Stanage in the Peak District, with Biddy and the Kellys. Prior to that weekend, Pat Kelly had been to Skye with Blanche Eden-Smith and Blanche's sister, and spent a wet week doing "ridges and peaks", including several ascents and descents on the Cioch.

One other interesting entry in Blanche Eden-Smith's diaries describes a Pinnacle Club meet in April 1921 in the Lake District. Apart from climbs on Scafell, Great End, Kern Knotts, Pavey Ark and Gimmer (some with the well-known Bentley Beetham), she refers to a "Pinnacle Club Committee Meeting on the Dress Circle", a large ledge on Great Gable. In attendance at that meet were Pat Kelly, Paddy Wells and Dr. Katie Corbett.

October 1921 saw another trip to Torver, for a Pinnacle Club meeting, which lasted only until lunchtime, as it left the afternoon free for climbing on the Coniston crags. Paddy Wells was again out on the crags. The following weekend, on Friday October 28th, H.M. Kelly gave a lecture to the Yorkshire Ramblers Club in Leeds, called "Recent New Climbing and Exploration around Wasdale". He stayed with Trilby and Biddy at their home in Moorland View, Ben Rhydding for the weekend, and on Saturday morning he climbed 'A' Climb (a one hundred foot Very Difficult route) at the Cow and Calf Rocks, Ilkley with Biddy. They then raced over to Almscliff Crag in Kelly's car, where they completed eight routes in the afternoon, and watched C.D. Frankland, a leading pioneer of Almscliff Crag, climb some of his routes. Sunday morning saw them up early to visit Rocky Valley on Ilkley Moor, where they climbed "lots of routes" including two new routes. On this day, Biddy and Kelly were accompanied by C.D. Frankland, who was a companion climber to Mabel Barker on later occasions. Biddy Wells was now mixing with some of the top climbers of the period, as too was Paddy as a member of both the Pinnacle and Fell and Rock clubs.

As if climbing in the U.K. was not enough of a challenge, in the summer of 1921 Paddy Wells took part in that year's Alpine Meet.

Lilian Bray, Dorothy Pilley and Paddy Wells formed a very strong climbing team who went guideless in the Alps, something that didn't take place very often in that period. They stayed at Saas, and climbed the Egginergrat, over 3500 metres, as their first exploit, arriving on the summit much sooner than expected. After a rest day, they attempted another 3600 metre peak, the Portjengrat, a harder route than two days previous, much to the chagrin of the local guides, who were getting used to men climbing guideless, but not women! By coincidence (or was it?), two men staying at the same hotel, Herbert R.C. Carr and John Hirst, also planned to climb the same rock ridge on that same day. Paddy Wells had never used crampons before this trip, so decided to leave them behind on this route, doing most of the leading on the rock pitches, but following Bray on snow and ice pitches. Bad weather, however, beat them back and a retreat in a thunderstorm involving several abseils was finally accomplished. They arrived back at the hotel after a nineteen-hour day! Incidentally, there is a wonderful description of this Alpine trip by Lilian Bray in The Pinnacle Club Journal number 1, of 1924. Paddy Wells and Lilian Bray were determined to complete the ascent another day, so after a couple of days the weather cleared sufficiently for another attempt. They set off with Paddy leading most of the route, had the mountain to themselves and successfully reached the summit. Lilian Bray praised Paddy's leading skills and route finding, both on the ascent and the descent, and they were back in the hotel in time for evening dinner. Paddy Wells was now extending her repertoire of climbs, and climbing guideless too. At the hotel, when they returned from their success, John Hirst was so impressed that he wrote in a later Rucksack Club Journal that "two undaunted damosels, scorning even the moral support of the mere male, returned to the attack, and departed for Ried with flying colours!"

So 1921 had again been a good year in many ways. The weather throughout the year had been mainly good, giving climbers and walkers a great opportunity for days on the crags and hills of both the U.K. and the Alps. Socially, too, Britain was slowly recovering from the after effects of the Great War: trains were running regularly from London to the Lakes and North Wales; car hire was now available for a few people in both mountain areas; accommodation was increasing and improving; new maps were being published; new guidebooks to climbing areas were appearing; and more and more people were able to afford, both in terms of time and money, to spend their weekends and holidays in the mountains. Climbing clubs produced journals containing details of new climbs and even new crags, with accounts of journeys and expeditions in the U.K. and abroad. Climbing and mountaineering was becoming more popular, more publicised and more accepted as a sport or pastime.

That year, Mabel Barker made her first lead as a climber when she led Kern Knotts Chimney. She also climbed in 1921 with Ralph Mayson, of Keswick photographic and postcard fame, prior to joining the Fell and Rock Club. On the formation of the Pinnacle Club, Mabel was very supportive of an all-women club, but did not join the club until 1931.

So to 1922, which again began with good weather, and several ladies were climbing in North Wales early in the year. There was also an informal dinner held by the Fell and Rock club at the Sun Inn, Coniston, on February 11th, to wish A.W. Wakefield and T.H. Somervell all the best as they were departing for Everest. John Hirst produced yet another of his famous songs, called "ENVOI", which was later published in the journal. Also in that FRCC journal was an excellent article by Eustace Thomas, called "A Lakeland Fell Circuit". Thomas and Wakefield had been the instigators of several long distance walks or runs, covering many of Lakeland's highest peaks within a set time, usually twenty-four hours. Inspiration indeed for the later runs of one Robert Graham, initiator of the now famous "Bob Graham Round", completed by several hundred mountaineers and fell runners to date.

Pat Kelly had arranged for the second A.G.M. of the Pinnacle Club to be held at Ogwen Cottage in Snowdonia on April 15th, 1922. Seventeen members were present, including the three Wells sisters. The Club reported that there were now fifty-nine members; had a healthy bank balance; a club handbook; and ten future meets planned. The committee also agreed to join the Advisory Council of British Mountaineering Clubs after a proposal by Lilian Bray, seconded by Paddy Wells. This was a council suggested by Geoffrey Winthrop Young and was the forerunner of the British Mountaineering Council. On the Saturday of the A.G.M., April 16th, members climbed on the Idwal Slabs, Milestone Buttress and on Tryfan. Also at this meet were six men from the Rucksack Club who were staying nearby, including Harry Kelly and J.H. Doughty. These men were led up some of the climbs by the women, and an enjoyable day was had by all. But the next day tragedy struck!

Sunday April 17th 1922 was a day that will always be remembered by members of the Pinnacle Club. Several of them had gone once again to climb on their favourite crag on the east face of Tryfan. The group of climbers was being watched by Pat Kelly who had decided not to climb that day as she felt unwell. After three ropes had complete three routes, the climbers were descending to the Heather Terrace. Trilby Wells was still above the terrace when she looked down to see a group of people around Pat Kelly, who was lying face down on the Terrace. Whether she had tripped or slipped no-one knew, but she had sustained serious head and facial injuries. A stretcher was brought up and Pat Kelly was taken down to the road and then taken to Bangor Hospital. H.M. Kelly, Pat's husband, and another Rucksack member J.V.T. Long, had been watching and encouraging the ladies as they climbed and so were present to accompany Pat Kelly down the mountain and then to the hospital. Trilby meanwhile descended to the terrace to be told that Pat had been found minus one shoe and no-one could find it. She must have lost it in the fall. Trilby carefully searched for the shoe to no avail. It was a mystery as to what had happened to the shoe and whether this had caused Pat to injure herself so seriously. But Trilby Wells was able to solve the riddle of the missing shoe sixty years later!

Blanche Eden-Smith, not present at the meet but a close friend of the Kellys, now journeyed up to North Wales, picking up Len Winthrop Young on the way and raced to Bangor Hospital to meet Harry Kelly and offer support. Pat was still unconscious at this time and would remain so for several days. So Len went home with her husband Geoffrey who had also been to see Pat Kelly, and then Blanche too travelled home. Everyone waited for news, and sadly at 9-00 a.m. on April 26th, 1922, Emily(Pat) Kelly passed away with her husband Harry and her friend Blanche (Gabriel) by her side. Both Eden-Smiths had travelled to Bangor when it was thought that Pat was near the end of her life. Gabriel stayed with Harry Kelly for the next few days, for the journey back to Manchester and for the cremation. When reading Gabriel's diaries, there is little reference to the actual events of the tragedy, apart from one simple entry dated April 26th: "We lost Pat"! Harry Kelly makes no reference at all in his diaries to the tragic death of his wife Pat. This was of course a tremendous shock and loss to the members of the Pinnacle Club and Trilby Wells spoke of this loss in her interviews. She described Pat Kelly as "a lovely lady, one of the best you could ever wish to meet", and said how unfortunate that someone so talented and brave on the rock should die of a simple fall on seemingly easy ground. There is a wonderful tribute to Pat Kelly on page 108 of the 1922 FRCC Journal, written by J.H. Doughty.

Paddy Wells leading in the guideless ascent of the Egginergrat in 1921.
(Photograph by Lilian Bray, from 'Pinnacle Club' by
Shirley Angell, Courtesy, The Pinnacle Club)

One mystery about 1922 remained. What had happened to Pat Kelly's missing shoe on the day of her death on Tryfan? Trilby Wells provided the answer. It seems that about six months after the accident, Trilby and Biddy Wells were climbing on Tryfan with Dr. and Mrs. Evans. Descending after completing their route, Dr. Evans found a climbing shoe, stuck between two rocks, trapped by one of its front nails. The party soon realised that this was the very shoe that Pat Kelly had lost. It appears that Pat's climbing shoes had been fitted with new nails, for her to try out that day for the first time. One of these nails must have caught on a rock as she descended, throwing her forward so violently that her foot had come out of her climbing shoe. The party who found the shoe buried it and all promised they would never tell of its discovery nor of its whereabouts, to avoid distressing Harry Kelly and the man who had given Pat the new nails. This information appears in Shirley Angell's history of the Pinnacle Club, when Trilby Wells told her the tale sixty years after the event. Trilby Wells felt that now Harry Kelly was dead, the story could finally be told.

The next 1922 entry in Gabriel's diary is on May 28th, and gives details of a trip to Laddow with Harry Kelly, Dr. Corbett and Len Winthrop Young. It is thought that this was Kelly's first outing to the crags since his wife's death. In Kelly's diaries, 1922 marks the first mention of 'G' as a climbing partner, and this was then to continue for many years. The Eden-Smiths were very kind to Kelly in the months after his wife's death, and he spent quite a lot of time at their home in Grange-over-Sands.

June and July saw Paddy Wells, with Gabriel and Kelly, in the Lakes. On several occasions Paddy was now also climbing and socialising with John Hirst, whom she had first met many years before and romance seemed to be in the air. Trilby later said that "it was obvious that he liked Paddy from the start and would chat to her on climbing days- always looking at her, watching her climb. But that didn't stop him helping all of us. She was his favourite though!" In the June meet, Paddy and Biddy Wells both climbed in Langdale, in Wasdale, on Pillar and again on Kern Knotts, while Paddy was elected Honorary Secretary of the Pinnacle Club in place of Pat Kelly.

However, another major event was to take place in July of 1922 affecting the Wells sisters On July 8th of that year, John Hirst married Annie (Paddy) Wells at the little church of St. Helen in Denton, near Ilkley. Once again, the Wells family had returned to the church where Paddy's parents were married and where each of the children were baptised. Wedding number 57 in the register of Marriages shows John Hirst, aged 38, widower and engineer, of Prestwich, Lancashire as the groom, the son of Edwin Hirst, builder. The bride was Annie Wells, aged 39, spinster and teacher, of Denton, daughter of Cooper Wells, a mason. The witnesses were E. Pryor and J. Wells, and the ceremony was conducted by the vicar, the Reverend S. Ross. Trilby and Biddy were of course in the congregation, as too were John Hirst's two young sons from his previous marriage: John Hunter Hirst born in Marple on November 18th, 1913, and James Pringle Hope Hirst, born in Marple on January 24th, 1916. It would appear that neither of the sons had been baptised, but this would be addressed in 1926. Paddy's mother Jane was also present, though Paddy's father Cooper had died in 1918.

Biddy had been leading climbs on Pillar and Scafell just before the wedding, including Jones' Route from Deep Ghyll by the arête. Within a few weeks of the wedding Biddy was back in the Lakes, in August, climbing Lower Kern Knotts Crack, with seven others! Biddy and party also spent time on the Y Boulder in Mosedale, as was the usual practice of the time. The 1923 FRCC Journal contained a description of Mosedale and said: "BOULDERS. There are at least two moderate-sized boulders in this valley which afford considerable amusement, apart from testing the climber's skill in the scrambles on them. The most famous of these is the Y BOULDER, situated about a mile above Ritson's Force, and easily recognised from a distance by a Y-shaped crack. There are nearly a score of routes up it of varying degrees of difficulty, one of which can be done feet foremost". Trilby spoke of the times she had visited the Y Boulder for scrambling, and for picnics on wet days or rest days. It is situated in a wonderful part of the Lake District, is well worth a visit and is certainly a great place for a picnic!

The 'Y Boulder', Mosedale, Lake District.

Trilby, with tongue in cheek, later suggested that the Y Boulder was so called because lots of Yorkshire people climbed on it! On this subject of bouldering, the 1916 FRCC Journal also mentions the sport of bouldering, in an article about Boulder Valley, Coniston: "On E. side of Old Man, below Low Water- 1hr's walk from Coniston. The Pudding Stone, 33 ft high, about 28 ft long- lots of routes on it. The Beck Stone; the Ridge Stone; The Inaccessible Boulder; The Pyramid". Strange to think that some modern day climbers think that "bouldering" is a relatively recent concept in climbing training, rather than a century old activity.

It was at Middle Row, in Wasdale, that the party stayed, as they did on several occasions. Always guaranteed a warm welcome, the Pinnacle Club ladies loved the atmosphere and hospitality of the place. Trilby spoke warmly about Middle Row, adding that Paddy and Biddy had stayed there more often than she had, especially in the early 1920s, before Trilby became a full member of the club.

Paddy meanwhile, now known as Mrs. Hirst, went off on honeymoon to Europe. There was no luxury city hotel nor beach holiday for Paddy and John though. This was to be a mountaineering honeymoon, spending much of their time in the Graian Alps, often using the Victor Emmanuel Hut and the Vittorio Sella Hut, in order to access several peaks. Trilby mentioned this during her interviews, and once again referred to the vicarious pleasure she and Biddy had when Paddy returned from honeymoon and told them all the tales of her adventures with her new husband on the Alpine peaks. Trilby was to visit the Graians herself in later years. At the same time Paddy was in the Alps, Dorothy Pilley was climbing Mont Blanc from the Italian side, as well as several other routes in the Mont Blanc area. Mabel Barker was also in the Alps that summer, climbing with Millican Dalton in Austria. This was to be her one and only Alpine visit, surprising because she was rapidly becoming one of the leading female climbers in Britain.

By the middle of August the Hirsts were back in Britain and Paddy attended the next committee meeting of the Pinnacle Club on August 21st 1922. As the newly elected Hon. Secretary, Paddy had to sign the minutes of the meeting and apparently wrote "Annie Wells", before remembering her new name and correcting it to "Annie Hirst"! Her husband John was busy producing a new songbook on behalf of the Rucksack Club. He had completed many Alpine seasons, had already climbed many of Scotland's Munros and was a popular character with members of several climbing clubs. He was a great singer and songwriter (as well as a composer of poems and ditties), his songs often being full of wit and gentle ridicule, but never unkind nor harmful. In fact, some of his songs apparently made fun of himself as well. With his great friend Harry Spilsbury, he often sang at meets and dinners, including at the Rucksack Club and FRCC dinners. He was also invited to address and sing at other club dinners as an honoured guest. In 1922 he produced "Songs of the Mountaineers" for the Rucksack Club, the full text of which can surprisingly be found on the internet, via the library of the University of Los Angeles! Interestingly, the songs have stood the test of time as some John Hirst songs appeared in an Alpine Club lecture in 2009 by Denis Gray and guitarist Paul Cherry. John Hirst was to become President of the Karabiner Mountaineering Club (after Fred Piggott and Eric Byrom) and also President of the Rucksack Club in 1944. His son John H. Hirst also became President of the latter club eighteen years later.

Paddy in 1922 had decided that she wanted to climb more on the Scottish peaks, and having been to Skye, she began "collecting" Munros with her husband. This was quite an undertaking and not something that many people had dared to attempt. To date, over four thousand people have completed the Munros, but in the 1920s it was a rare undertaking. It would take Paddy, and John, until 1947 to achieve their aim. John had to repeat many of the peaks he had already climbed before meeting Paddy, but it kept them occupied for the next twenty-five years!

Away from mountaineering, in the Whitsuntide holidays of 1922 the Yorkshire Ramblers had decided to put a winch into the huge pot-hole near Ingleborough, in the Yorkshire Dales, called Gaping Ghyll. As soon as they heard of the plan Trilby and Biddy were desperate to go down the pot and duly turned up with several fellow Pinnacle Club members. So, each in turn, down they went, thus becoming the first women ever to descend the pot-hole. In the 1969-70 Pinnacle Club Journal Trilby wrote about their visit underground, stating that at the time of writing she was the “only one left”. This was another “first” for the two Wells sisters.

Photo of the first women ever to descend Gaping Ghyll, 1922.
L-R Catherine Corbett, Dorothy Thompson,
Dorothy Evans, Biddy Wells, Trilby Wells.

Thus ended 1922. Paddy was married, had again climbed in the Alps, was now Secretary of the Pinnacle Club and had started her quest to climb the Munros. Biddy had really extended her climbing experiences in the Lake District and on gritstone, and Trilby too had completed more and more rock climbs both on the Pennine grit and in the Lakes and Wales. 1923 followed a similar pattern. Paddy represented the Pinnacle Club at the Ladies Dinner of the Fell and Rock Club on January 26th at the Hotel Metropole, before journeying to Scotland with husband John for a short holiday. The Wells sisters attended several of the meets in Derbyshire (Stanage and Windgather), at Laddow and in the Lakes. For example, Trilby climbed Eagles Nest Direct at Whitsun with Dr. and Mrs. Evans. They also began to attend the occasional FRCC meet.

In November, the three sisters attended the first Manchester dinner at the Albion Hotel, and went on to climb at Stanage the next day. Shirley Angell's history of the Pinnacle Club notes that these early dinners were followed by a varied session of entertainment, such as songs, sketches and music. Trilby talked so much about this in her interviews, saying that the same 'entertainment' often occurred in the evenings at club meets in Wales and the Lakes. Trilby and Biddy were both adept at writing and performing short plays, usually witty and related to recent events, as well as singing and dancing; they did the same thing with church and local groups back home in Ben Rhydding.

Finally, 1923 was also the year that Mabel Barker had first met the great Yorkshire climber Claude Frankland, who had put up lots of routes on his favourite crag, Almscliff. Frankland's Green Crack remains a favourite even for today's generation of climbers. C.D. Frankland was the headteacher of Sweet Street School in Leeds, and lived close enough to Wharfedale to make regular visits to the local crags. Trilby and Biddy had met him on several occasions, and in 1924 took the Winthrop Youngs to Almscliff to watch him climb.

THE MIDDLE YEARS OF THE 1920'S

1924 was a special year for Paddy Wells as she was elected President of the Pinnacle Club at the A.G.M., held in Coniston. Biddy, too, was elected to office becoming Honorary Secretary in place of Paddy. All three sisters were climbing regularly, and Trilby was preparing to apply for full membership of the Pinnacle Club. During the first three months of that year Paddy and Biddy had climbed in the Lakes, and also visited Dow Crag during the A.G.M. Meet. Two new "Red Guides" were out, published by the FRCC in 1922 and 1923 and which are nowadays a rare item for collectors of mountaineering literature. The first guide, "Doe Crags and Climbs around Coniston" by G.S. Bower, priced at 2/3d (11p) was warmly welcomed by all climbers, and must have been in the possession of Pinnacle Club members in 1924. So too the second guide, "Pillar Rock" by H.M. Kelly, priced 2/6d 'post free' (12p). There were three more guides to come out over the next three years. These guides contained information on access to the crags, details of the routes, excellent photographs and diagrams, and a list of first ascents. However, Bower did write at the start of the first guide that "there is no need to describe the situation of 'The Crags' to any member of the Fell and Rock Club", so well known was Dow Crag. There was also a comprehensive description of Boulder Valley near Coniston. Kelly's guide to Pillar Rock was nearly twice the size of Bower's, and in it Kelly praises the help given in its production by Blanche Eden-Smith and others. Kelly had spent many days at Middle Row in Wasdale while working on the guide, and he and his late wife Pat and the Eden-Smiths are prominent in many of the first ascent details.

The Fell & Rock Memorial on Great Gable.
Trilby Wells attended the unveiling of the Memorial in 1924.

At Whitsun 1924, a special occasion was to take place in the Lake District. A commemorative service was held near the summit of Great Gable, to unveil a memorial tablet, and over five hundred people attended. The date was June 8th, and in her interviews Trilby described her being there along with her two sisters. In a taped interview with Mike Gibbons, a local Wharfedale mountaineer,

Trilby explained how the weather on the day was wet and windy- "a horrible day". Before the parson could dedicate the tablet to the fallen of the Great War he had to fight with his surplice in the wind. "I had to help him put it on!" Trilby added. The ceremony is described in detail in an article in the 1924 Fell and Rock Journal. The three Wells sisters spent the Whitsun week climbing in the Wasdale area though Trilby gave no hint as to the routes completed. All three were teachers and so the meet coincided with a school holiday. Biddy and Trilby travelled from Ben Rhydding and Paddy came up from Manchester to join them, along with husband John. Dr. A.W. Wakefield, Club President, unveiled the plaque, Geoffrey Winthrop Young made a short speech, and Godfrey Solly read a psalm. Then all the names of the fallen club members were read out and buglers played the "Last Post". Trilby described it as a very moving occasion despite the weather.

Many famous mountaineers were present on Great Gable, and it is interesting to note the people that the three Ben Rhydding sisters were associated with, during social and climbing occasions. People such as W. Heaton Cooper, I.A. Richards, C.F. Holland, Herbert Carr, Charles Evans, George Mallory, Fred Piggott, Bentley Beetham, George Samson, George Basterfield and the Abraham brothers-the list is like a whos-who of mountaineering greats. Trilby mentioned Evans, Heaton Cooper, Richards and Carr in her interviews, as all being a real support to women climbers at the time.

Meanwhile, 1924 saw Pinnacle Club members in the Pyrenees, Norway, the Alps and the Kaisergebirge. Paddy and her sisters continued to climb and walk in the U.K., Paddy also visiting Scotland with her husband. A new song by John Hirst, called simply "Fell and Rock", was written and it was to appear in the 1925 FRCC Journal.

1924 also saw the start of a climbing partnership between C.D.

Frankland and Mabel Barker which lasted for three years. In October of that year Mabel was at Almscliff Crag with Frankland and they also visited the Cow and Calf Rocks at Ilkley in December. They were simply exploring the Cow and Calf area for new routes, because most of the routes at Ilkley were at nearby Rocky Valley, and it was to be a while before routes were first climbed at the quarry next to the Cow and Calf. Mabel and Frankland also climbed together in the Lakes that year.

At home, Trilby and Biddy were still teaching, and were still active members of St. John's Church in Ben Rhydding. They began singing in the choir too, and serving on committees- something they continued to do for many years.

On January 10th 1925, Paddy arranged a musical evening to follow the Manchester dinner of the Pinnacle Club; and at Easter there was another North Wales meet, where climbs were completed on Clogwyn y Person, Tryfan and Lliwedd. This was the year too that Dorothy Pilley left the U.K. for a two-year climbing trip around the world with I.A. Richards. A tragic accident also occurred in 1925 when Herbert Carr, friend of the Wells sisters, fell off a climb in Cwm Glas in Snowdonia. His companion was pulled off the crag and sadly killed. Carr was not found for forty eight hours, but despite terrible injuries he survived.

Harry Kelly and Blanche Eden-Smith also continued their climbing partnership in 1925 in the Lake District, sometimes joined by Biddy and Paddy, before going off to Norway again, while Lilian Bray again visited the Kaisergebirge. Trilby meanwhile had finally decided to upgrade her membership of the Pinnacle Club. In her original application form (number 41 at the time) for Associate Membership on March 25th 1921, she had described her previous experience as "Mountaineering in N. Wales and Lake District- also on Pennines". Thus she had not deemed herself capable of becoming a full member like her two sisters, but by 1925 Trilby Wells had climbed enough routes to qualify. She had climbed lots of routes in Yorkshire at Almscliff and Ilkley, and at Laddow, and now had experience of routes in the Lakes and Wales. Finally, Trilby had led a girl called Maisie Gregg up a route; then later led an unknown man up a route. The route is not known but must have been of a reasonable standard to enable Trilby to be accepted as a "Full Member". So 1925 was about gaining experience for Trilby and she finally became a Full member in 1926.

Mabel Barker visited Skye in August 1925 with Claude Frankland, as well as completing a notable ascent on Scafell. Again in August, the weather was fine, and ideal for an attempt on the now-famous Central Buttress, which had only had three previous ascents. The pair completed the fourth ascent, this being the first ascent by a woman- a remarkable achievement which was recorded and favourably commented on in all the mountaineering journals of the time. This was to be Mabel's 'swansong' for a while, as in September 1925 she moved to Montpellier in France. She had also been offered a job in America, but turned it down, as her real ambition, after gaining more experience in France, was to open her own school in the Lake District- a school which Trilby and Biddy Wells were later to visit.

So to 1926 and a special start to the year for Paddy Hirst, now starting her third year as President of the Pinnacle Club. On January 14th 1926, Paddy gave birth to a daughter, a step-sister to John Hirst's two sons by his first marriage. Trilby and Biddy were of course delighted at the news and soon, on March 14th of that year, once again the Wells sisters returned to the tiny Church of St. Helen at Denton, near Ilkley. Paddy and John travelled from their home in Marple, Cheshire, for the christening of their daughter, Joyce. She was christened by the same vicar who had married them, Reverend S. Ross. At the same service, John Hirst's two sons, John Hunter Hirst, born 1913, and James Pringle Hope Hirst, born 1916, were also christened. This was yet another link between the Wells family and Denton Church.

The Easter meet of that year was planned for Torver again, and despite the Depression and the general Strike in that year, Pinnacle Club members were still able to get away for meets. A very special occasion of 1926 was the "party" on top of Pillar, in the Lakes, to celebrate the centenary of John Atkinson's first ascent of Pillar; the party was attended by climbers and walkers from many U.K. destinations. The group included both Trilby and Biddy Wells, along with other Pinnacle Club members. Well into her eighties, Trilby had quite vivid memories of that day and of the previous memorial service on Great Gable. It was another example of an occasion in mountaineering history when one or more of the Ben Rhydding sisters were in attendance.

Summer arrived and on July 1st came one of the truly great climbing events of that era- the first ascent of Moss Ghyll Grooves by Harry Kelly, Blanche Eden-Smith and J.B. Kilshaw. Kelly had spent many days over a long period of time, surveying the route from different vantage points, climbing parts of the route and working out the correct line. In the end, an hour and a half was sufficient for the trio to successfully make the first ascent of what was to become a great classic. Blanche, or G. as she was then known, wrote an article about Moss Ghyll Grooves in the 1926 Fell and Rock journal. Soon afterwards, Kelly and G. accompanied Len Winthrop Young on a trip to Norway, to celebrate the fiftieth anniversary of Cecil Slingsby's (Len's father) first ascent of Skagastolstind in 1876. In her eighties, Trilby Wells spoke of the pleasure on certain evenings at Pinnacle

Club meets, when people such as G. would tell of their foreign exploits; and how later even the three Wells sisters had a few tales to tell of Alpine adventures.

Mabel Barker meanwhile had returned from France in the summer of 1926 in time to accompany Claude Frankland and others to the Isle of Skye. From a camp at the outlet of Loch Coruisk into Loch Scavaig, (surely one of the most dramatic and scenic situations in Britain), Mabel and Claude ascended to the summit of Gars Bheinn by 7-00 a.m. in mist rain and wind. In continuous mixed weather of rain, sun and mist, they sheltered several times from heavy hail storms. Undeterred, they continued to move rapidly, finally reaching the end of the Cuillin Ridge at the summit of Sgurr nan Gillean by 8-30 p.m. They returned to Scavaig by 1-00 a.m., completing the first traverse of the ridge by a woman. However, as she was accompanied by a man, there had still been no ridge traverse by an all-female party. This was of relevance to the Wells sisters, and it became an ambition for Trilby and Biddy Wells over the next couple of years. Alas, Claude Frankland would not live to witness this as he died in a mountain accident in 1927.

Members of the Pinnacle Club, whilst hearing of the exploits of others, were also planning their own adventures, and the first Alpine Meet was arranged for that summer. This was to be Trilby Wells' introduction to Alpine mountaineering, and what an introduction it was! Sam Hall, who had just soloed the "Tour of Mont Blanc" (in itself a marvellous feat), met Trilby, Harriet Turner and leader of the group Dr. Corbett in Argentiere. (Note that Katie/Catherine Corbett is always referred to as Dr. Corbett or simply Corbett). In poor weather they visited the Mer de Glace and Montenvers for acclimatising, and spent a day in Chamonix. The next day they climbed the Buet as a training climb. Sam Hall was becoming affected by the altitude, so dropped out of future forays, but Trilby Wells and the other two completed the Three Cols Route with a guide, before visiting the Brevent and La Perseverance. Older sister Paddy joined Trilby on the last venture, as she had just travelled from Arolla where she had been climbing guideless. Paddy was having an excellent year, completing the ascents of several Munros in Scotland and visiting the Alps with husband John, as well as joining up with Trilby in Argentiere.

So as a first Alpine adventure for Trilby, this was becoming quite an incredible experience for the thirty-seven year old from Ben Rhydding. But the best was yet to come- an ascent of the highest peak in the European Alps, Mont Blanc! Sam Hall had by now recovered sufficiently to attempt the climb, and so she joined Corbett and Trilby Wells on the ascent. They were extremely lucky with the snow and the weather and made excellent progress until just below the summit, where Dr. Corbett realised she could not go any further as the altitude began to take effect on her. She did not want to jeopardise the chances of the others making the summit so encouraged the two of them to continue without her. Trilby Wells soon stood on the top of Mont Blanc, on August 3rd,1926, alongside Sam Hall. When questioned in the 1980s about her remarkable first Alpine visit and her ascent of Mont Blanc, Trilby spoke with great pride about her arrival on the summit, saying that her ice-axe from the ascent was now in the possession of a friend in Ilkley. Sadly, no-one has since been able to locate the missing ice-axe.

The three ladies descended to Chamonix, and Trilby and Sam Hall were applauded by the local guides, before being presented with certificates to verify their ascent. Trilby's certificate now hangs in the Emily Kelly Hut at Cwm Dyli- a fitting tribute to a tough Yorkshire lady. People meeting the three Wells sisters in later life would hardly suspect that these three slightly-built, aged ladies were such tough and rugged mountaineers in their younger days.

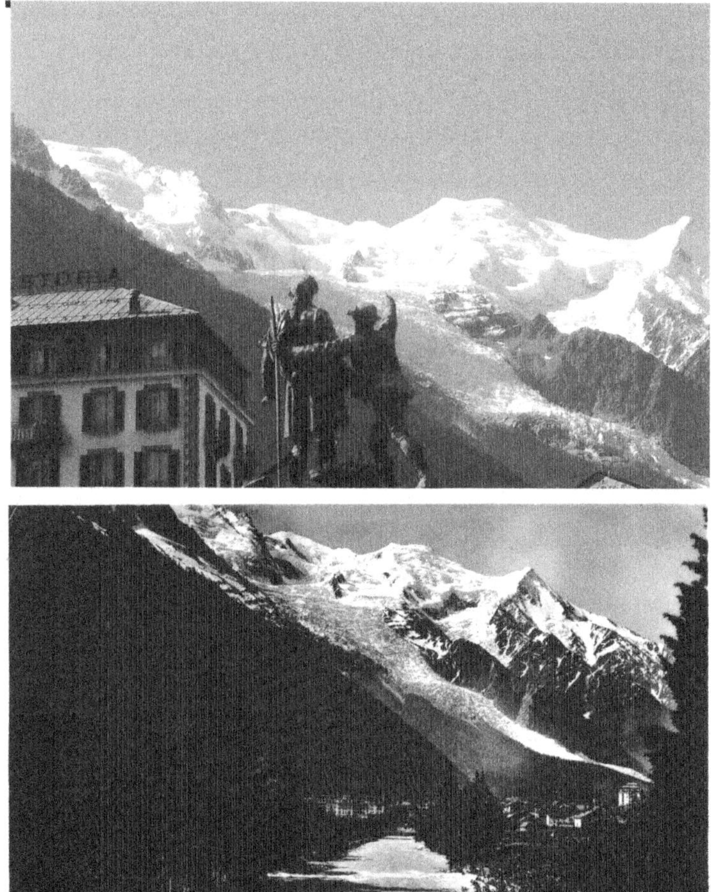

Chamonix and Mont Blanc, now and then.
Start and finish of Trilby's ascent in 1928.

Two further events ended 1926: Dorothy Pilley married I.A. Richards on December 31st in Honolulu during their two-year round-the-world climbing trip, and Paddy Wells' time in office was coming to an end, after three years as President of the Pinnacle Club. Lilian Bray would take over the President's role for the years 1927-29.

During 1927 all three Wells sisters climbed in the Lakes, North Wales and at Laddow. There was also a very wet but very enjoyable Skye meet at Whitsun, arranged by the Pinnacle Club. Six members stayed at Mrs. Macrae's at Glen Brittle, wanting to "do the ridge". They spent a few days exploring the ridge, to acquaint themselves with the twists and turns, the ascents and descents, etc. as route finding can be very difficult if poor weather occurs. Trilby and Biddy had previously visited Skye so had a little prior knowledge of the ridge. They also climbed up and down the North side of the Thearlaich Dubh gap, and did Collie's Ledge on Sgurr Mhic Coinnich. Finally, they left a dump of food near the Inaccessible Pinnacle, and food and extra clothing between Bidean and Caisteal. There were great deliberations between Trilby, Biddy, Bray and Corbett about what was the best time to start, and they eventually agreed on a 5-00 a.m. departure. However, rain at Glen Brittle and snow on the ridge meant a return to bed! The next day, with the weather improving, they left Mrs. Macrae's at 9-00 a.m. each carrying a small amount of food, one shared bottle of water, and a thin mackintosh each in case of rain.

They crossed the moor and climbed up Gars Bheinn to where the ridge proper begins, and made very good progress as far as the Thearlaich Dubh gap, where Lilian Bray roped the other three down the climb into the Gap, as Bray was the only one who knew how to abseil properly! She then abseiled into the Gap, whereupon Biddy Wells (as so often the case) led the pre-practised climb up the other side of the Gap. This was completed in a storm of hail and rain, with a wind whistling through the Gap, giving the whole party a few cautious moments and some frozen fingers. Even more wintry showers followed as they made steady progress along the ridge as far as the Inaccessible Pinnacle. Once again, instead of scrambling up the long, easier but exposed rib and abseiling off the top of the Pinnacle, the party had to reverse the long upward route, before stopping for a rest near the Pinnacle. By now it was nearly 9-00 p.m. and the party was hit by a heavy storm of rain and hail. The four huddled together in shelter to eat some of their provisions left there earlier, before continuing as far as Sgurr a Greadaidh by 11 p.m. Tiredness had begun to overtake them by now, so they agreed to rest for a few hours. It must be remembered that they had already covered several miles and the terrain is extremely rough and demanding. Tiredness can easily lead to a slip or worse in this event, and the ridge is no place for the faint hearted. Lacking shelter in such an exposed and windswept part of the ridge, they huddled in pairs and tried in vain to sleep. They shivered throughout the night, and took it in turns to get up and jump about waving their arms to try and warm themselves up. By 3-00 a.m. and the slow return of daylight, they were up and eating a little breakfast. The shared water bottle had frozen solid, even though it had been in a rucksack all night, so they had nothing to drink. After proceeding along the ridge for another half an hour they became enveloped in thick mist and cloud, and the ice-covered rocks became slippery and dangerous. Their pace had slowed considerably and they eventually lost their way along the ridge. All agreed it was time to abandon the attempt and they dropped down below the mist, heading back to Mrs. Macrae's. By 6-30 a.m. they were "back home", sipping tea, realising it was the end of that year's attempt on the Skye Ridge. It was good experience however, and would stand them in good stead next time they attempted the ridge. Though it was June, the weather is so unpredictable and changeable on the ridge and night-time temperatures can still be quite low. But Trilby and Biddy Wells would not be beaten and vowed to make another attempt in 1928.

Similar fortitude was shown by Geoffrey Winthrop Young that summer as, despite losing a leg, he was able to complete the ascents of the Riffelhorn and of Monte Rosa in the Alps. However, the tragic death of Claude Frankland occurred on July 31st of that year in an accident on Great Gable. He was described in the FRCC Journal as "without equal among cragsmen" and the "finest exponent" of crag climbing.

In the Autumn of 1927, the three Wells sisters organised a Pinnacle Club Yorkshire Meet, at Almscliff Crag, between Otley and Harrogate. They were able to hire a small bungalow at Castley, near Pool-in-Wharfedale, close to the river. Once again, Trilby later spoke of the "Yorkshire Meets" in her interviews, and she mentioned Castley as a favourite venue. However, several other venues in Yorkshire were used on different occasions, and these Yorkshire meets continued through to the latter decades of the twentieth century. At Castley, the Wells sisters did the catering and organised the evening entertainment too. Not surprising as by now Biddy and Trilby had joined local amateur dramatic and operatic societies in the Menston and Ilkley areas.

A new member, Marjorie Wood, joined the Pinnacle Club at the Castley meet, and remained a member for the rest of her life. She knew Biddy and Trilby prior to joining the club, and had climbed with them at Almscliff. She described the Wells sisters as having made a valuable contribution to the early days of the Pinnacle Club.

Towards the end of the year, on October 8th, 1927, a special dinner was arranged at the Windermere Hydro. The FRCC Journal describes a "coming-of-age" dinner (21 years), with representatives from several clubs, including the Pinnacle Club. There was a special three-tiered cake topped with a model of Napes Needle, and John Hirst composed a song for the occasion called "The Rock and Fell". In speeches, several members who had passed away that year were mentioned, including H.P. Cain (while walking in Langdale), and the Almscliff climber Claude Frankland. Paddy Hirst and her two sisters were at the dinner, though Biddy and Trilby actually signed in as N. (Nellie) Wells and E. (Emily) Wells. Other clubs represented included the Rucksack Club, Yorkshire Ramblers and the Alpine and Ladies Alpine Clubs. Speakers included Eustace Thomas, Ashley Abraham and Len Winthrop Young. Len's speech went down a treat as she proposed the toast of "kindred clubs" which she said were "like a family": the Alpine Club was the grandfather; Uncle Rucksack; Uncles and Aunts from Scottish Clubs and the Yorkshire Ramblers; an elder sister the Ladies Alpine Club; and finally the Pinnacle Club barely out of school!

The following day climbs and walks were completed on Dow Crags, Gimmer, Pavey Ark, Saddleback, Helvellyn and on the Kentmere Fells. It is not known on which fell the Wells sisters spent their day. Thus the Pinnacle Club was now a major player in the mountaineering circles of the 1920s, and the Wells sister were three of its leading characters.

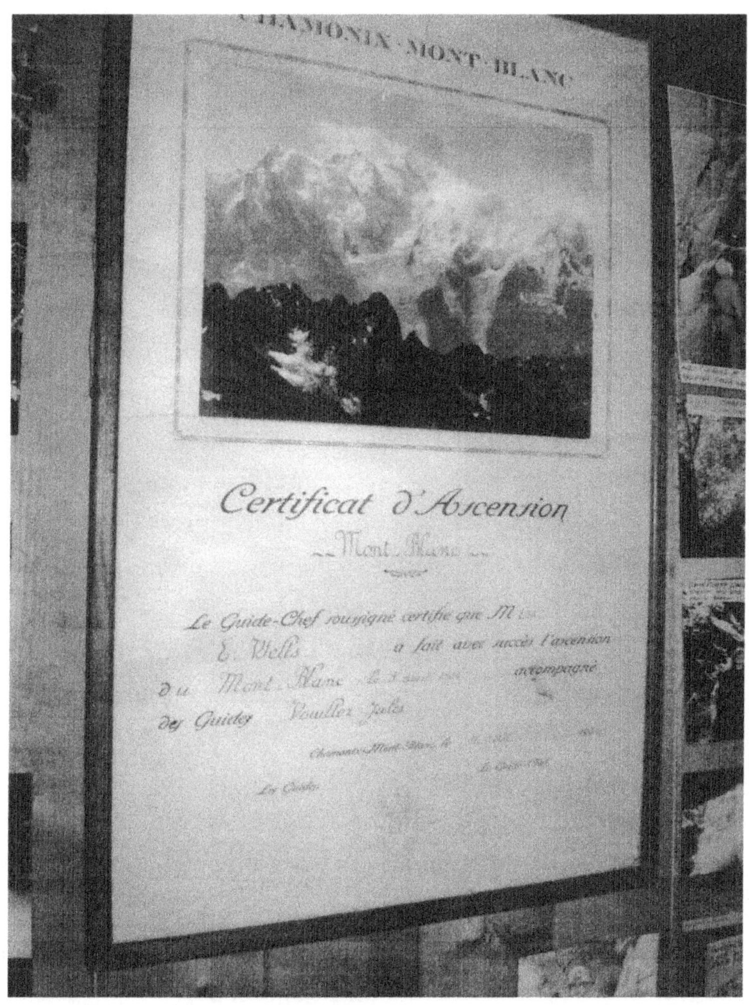

Trilby Wells' certificate for climbing Mont Blanc.

1928 – A VERY SPECIAL YEAR

1928 was to become a memorable year for two of our three Wells sisters, Trilby and Biddy, who continued to live at Moorland View in Ben Rhydding. They continued with their teaching careers at the Margaret Macmillan School, and regularly attended church several times each week. They were also involved in local amateur dramatics, but also spent as much time as possible on the crags and mountains. Trilby spoke of 1928 as being one of her favourite years, as she again achieved success both at home and abroad. Older sister Paddy was also climbing with husband John, and living at Bowden Lane, Marple, in Cheshire. The pair continued to climb the occasional Munro in Scotland, slowly adding to their list of ascents, as well as rock climbing together.

The year started with a Pinnacle Club Dinner on January 7th in Manchester, attended by all three Wells sisters. Harry Kelly and Blanche Eden-Smith climbed together in the Lakes on regular weekends, sometimes joined by Biddy and Trilby, up to Easter, though the weather was not kind to them on several occasions. In April, Kelly put up a new route on Pillar called Grooved Wall. Mabel Barker, too, was fast becoming well-known for her climbing exploits and on March 31st she also put up a new route on Castle Rock of Triermain in the Lakes with Graham Macphee.

Easter weekend brought a Pinnacle Club meet in North Wales, which included the AGM, where Biddy resigned as Secretary. Later, on July 3rd, Mabel Barker and Macphee were back on Castle Rock, climbing two more new routes- Slab Climb and Scoop and Crack Climb. Trilby mentioned later that she and Biddy had "bumped into"

Mabel Barker on a couple of occasions in Langdale and elsewhere, and on one of these occasions had been invited by Mabel to visit her later. This they did.

Whitsun proved to be a very busy period in several parts of the country. Geoffrey Winthrop Young had journeyed to Wales with his wife Len, and had walked up to "Cloggy" (Clogwyn Du'r Arddu) on the flanks of Snowdon. After swimming in the lake, they both watched the first ascent of Longland's Climb, a major event in the history of this famous crag. There is an excellent account of the day in "The Black Cliff", a history of Clogwyn Du'r Arddu by Crew and Soper.

Meanwhile, the Pinnacle Club Whitsun Meet was again held at Glenbrittle, on Skye, with four ladies arriving on the Saturday in the mist and rain. Weather on Skye is always very changeable, and one is very lucky to experience a long spell of decent weather on the island. Opportunities to climb or to attempt the ridge must be taken whenever they occur, and being "in situ" is always a good idea. Thus, Lilian Bray, Katie Corbett, Biddy Wells and Trilby Wells arrived at Mrs. Macrae's house, one of the few buildings in Glenbrittle at the time. At the end of the lane was a small collection of buildings: the Post Office, the Lodge and Mrs. Campbell's farm where many of the early pioneers had lodged. Mrs. Macrae's was nearby.

The first complete traverse of the Cuillin Ridge of Skye had been completed in 1911 by Messrs Shadbolt and Mclaren in seventeen hours, and T.H. Somervell (of Everest fame) was the first to solo the complete route in 1914. On August 26th, 1926, Mabel Barker had become the first woman to traverse the ridge, starting and finishing at Coruisk, in twenty hours and in bad weather. However, she had been accompanied by a man, C.D. Frankland, of Almscliff fame, and there was a burning desire amongst the ladies of the Pinnacle Club to achieve the first all-female traverse. The 1926 attempt is mentioned in the 1935 SMC guide to the Isle of Skye, as is the 1928 traverse here described.

Loch Coruisk from the Skye Ridge, traversed by Trilby and Biddy Wells in 1928.

To be the first all-female party would indeed be a tremendous feat, and from the outset Bray, Biddy and Trilby were determined to be the first. A wonderful article by Lilian Bray in the 1927-28 Pinnacle Club Journal describes the preparation and the traverse in great detail. Nearly sixty years later, in conversation with the author (who had himself just soloed the ridge), Trilby was quite animated and proud of her achievement. She was able to describe clearly, yet very modestly, how exciting the whole venture had been. She said that though her writing was no longer legible, her "memory was still very good!" The 1935 SMC guide has a short paragraph about their traverse but then goes on to describe the Cuillin Ridge thus:

"Probably the best British rock climbing expedition, about 10,000 feet of ascent and descent… exhausting and strenuous. You need to be fit to attempt it. Navigation and route finding is difficult even in good weather… also carry water as lack of refuelling spots on the ridge." So Trilby, Biddy and Bray knew what they were undertaking, and had spoken earlier to several people who had climbed on Skye and who had been on the ridge, including Harry Kelly, John Hirst and Mabel Barker. Trilby also said that she had met T.H. Somervell at the 1927 Fell and Rock Dinner at the Hydro in Windermere, and he had spoken to her about the ridge and his traverse. Trilby fondly remembered the traverse as one of her best times on the mountains, despite the heat and the lack of water en route, particularly so as she was accompanied by "my sister and best friend". She also said they "bivouacked somewhere, but didn't sleep very well!" Each time they had met, the Wells sisters had spent the last twelve months talking about the ridge, ever since their failed attempt, thereby increasing their determination to complete it in 1928.

Their first few days on Skye were spent preparing for the attempt. All three had been to Skye before and had lots of previous knowledge of the ridge. On the Sunday, despite mist and light rain, they again made two dumps of food on the ridge, (but sadly no water bottles) before Monday's rain brought about a rest day. For the next few days, the weather forecast was good, and the attempt was to begin on the Wednesday morning at 2.30 a.m. By the time they reached Gars Bheinn it was already bright and sunny and quite warm, with no wind and clear skies. Both Biddy and Trilby had learned to abseil competently since the last attempt and so the Thearlaich Dubh Gap proved an easier obstacle this time. By midday they had reached An Stac, in searing heat, and soon they reached the Inaccessible Pinnacle. Up the easier long rib, and an abseil down the steep short side, saved a lot of time, even though they had now been on the go for nine and a half hours. They retrieved their food dump from near to the Pinnacle, but were unable to eat much as they were so dry and hot. A little fruit was sufficient. They had no water left however, and on the Skye ridge there are very few opportunities (perhaps only one or two, and only if you know where they are) to obtain any water. By 12.30, as the temperature rose, they were again on the move but suffering terribly with the heat; and without a hat for shade, Bray wore a handkerchief on her head to alleviate sunburn. The heat made them slow considerably, and in her article in the Pinnacle Club Journal, Bray jokingly states that all three determined that their next climbing holiday would be in Holland!

Several hours ensued, and the high temperatures slowed the party even more, until approaching Bruach na Frithe at 9.00 p.m. they realised they must stop to rest. They found a sloping piece of ground to lie down on, and prepared to eat the single lemon they had been carrying all day, Bray describes what happened next as "tragedy"- someone dropped the lemon, it bounced down the slope and disappeared down the mountain, before they had a chance to even moisten their lips. They were apparently speechless.

The night was beautiful- starry sky, light breeze, total silence. At least, it was until they began to stir soon after 3.00 a.m. Still terribly thirsty, they departed their 'bivouac' at 3.30, soon reaching the summit of Bruach na Frithe, where they found three apples kindly placed there by friends. Biddy and Trilby could eat nothing, their mouths so dry. Ignoring Naismith's Route on the Bhasteir Tooth, they scrambled round to the other side, climbed the remaining few summits, and finally the end was in sight. The western ridge of Sgurr nan Gillean was completed and they continued down the tourist path, with no water on one of the hottest days of the year. They did manage some mouthfuls of water from burns as they followed the path down to Sligachan, before finally sitting down to numerous pots of tea at 11.00 a.m.

This was undoubtedly a remarkable feat- the first complete traverse of the Cuillin Ridge by an all-female party. Those of us who have experienced the traverse in the latter part of the twentieth century can well understand the immensity of their achievement. Trilby and Bray wore Kletterschue on their feet and were comfortable in these lightweight boots. Biddy's, however, did not fit her so well, so she wore her big boots. They carried a small rucksack between them and a half-weight rope, for the short upward pitches and the abseils on the ridge. Also, a small rope sling from which they abseiled down the Thearlaich Dubh Gap, and then left behind. In later interviews, Trilby was asked about the two days on the ridge, and though extremely proud, she refused to make a big issue of her achievement. She did admit, however, that it was a big mistake to carry so little water and that they should have cached some bottles on the ridge beforehand. The Skye guide mentions our three ladies and describes their traverse as a "noteable expedition".

Finally, after thirty hours of mountaineering and reinforced by several pots of tea, our three adventurers found there was now no car available at Sligachan to ferry them back to base. So the three of them set off to walk back to Glenbrittle over the moor, a mere distance of ten more miles! Three sunburnt faces peered through the window at Mrs. Macrae's at 4.30 p.m. to announce their success.

Trilby and Biddy Wells had achieved a remarkable feat and returned home to Ben Rhydding pleased with their Skye jaunt and in buoyant mood. They now had a few more weeks at school before the summer holidays beckoned and immediately Trilby started planning her next mountain venture. This was to be the second Pinnacle Club

Alpine Meet, and the aim was to climb guideless. Four women were to go on the meet, yet another example of climbing "sans homme" and without local guides. Trilby was excited as the end of term loomed ever closer and soon she travelled by train to London to meet Dr. Corbett, from where they set off on July 27th for the Channel. On the ferry they were joined by Dr. Taylor, and the three then travelled by train to Aosta, via Turin. After a relaxing night in Aosta, they continued by bus to the tiny village of Villeneuve, before a five-hour walk up to the Eau Rousse Hut. At Valsavaranche they met Bray, and the party was complete. There had been a severe drought in the area for two months and all the locals, much to the annoyance of the climbers, were praying for rain!

Next day, the four set off for the Victor Emmanuel Hut for a week's stay, where they were fortunate to obtain a four-bunked room for the duration. At eight thousand feet up in the mountains, it is a good place to acclimatise, even if washing in the nearby glacier lake was rather cool. Their first foray was to the Gran Paradiso at over 4,000 metres, leaving the hut at 4.30 a.m. and summiting successfully at 9.30 a.m. They were the first English women to reach the summit guideless- yet another "first" for Trilby Wells.

Next, Trilby, Corbett and Taylor were to attempt the Ciarforon and the Monciair, both about 3,500 metres. Bray, who had previously climbed them, offered advice but decided to remain at the hut. So the three ladies reluctantly decided to hire a local guide. Both summits were reached, but Trilby was very concerned on both ascent and descent of the Monciair by the loose shale on the route, which constantly moved and slid down on people below. On the descent they were hit by a passing lightning storm, and were forced to throw down their ice axes and move well away from them to shelter in some rocks. Eventually the storm moved on and they were able to continue the descent, cross the glacier and return to the hut.

After a rest day, Trilby and the other three ladies climbed the Punta di Ceresole, led by Bray. They had only one serious ice pitch, and scrambled up most of the route unroped, reaching steep ice near to the summit, where they cut steps. On the descent, Trilby demonstrated her ability to abseil down the rock pitch, but after Bray had followed her down, the rope became jammed. Luckily, they were able to free it after much effort, thus avoiding cutting Taylor's rope in two!

Another guideless ascent followed, this time up the Tresenta, which at over 3,500 metres Trilby found rather easy. At night in the hut, Trilby had to keep patching her trousers as they wore away on the rough rock, and eventually there were more patches than trousers! The effort of climbing for a week also had an effect on Lilian Bray who apparently lost a stone in weight.

The four ladies returned to the valley next day, from where Dr. Taylor left for an attempt on the Matterhorn. Trilby enjoyed a couple of lazy days, swimming in the local lakes and strolling along local paths. Dr. Corbett, too, now had to leave the group to return home, so Trilby and Bray set off on foot to Nivolet, and then the next day to Ceresole, where they booked into the Grand Hotel. What a contrast to the mountain huts of the previous week. With the hotel full of smartly-dressed Italians, Trilby worried about how two scruffy mountaineers could look half-decent at dinner. Converting their nighties into "dresses" and buying cheap cardigans locally, they somehow survived the ordeal of the dining room and thankfully left the hotel next morning. They returned to Nivolet for the night, having abandoned their original idea of visiting Val d'Isere, and then continued on to Valsavaranche. Finally, they did manage to get transport to Val d'Isere where they met Dorothy Pilley/ Richards and her husband who had just made the first ascent of the North Ridge of the Dent Blanche.

Bray and Trilby were now ready for home, and that same evening they departed for England. Three days later Trilby was back home in Ben Rhydding, and soon preparing for a new term at school.

Sadly, we cannot end 1928 without mentioning the death of a local man, one of Britain's great mountaineers, W.C. Slingsby. A resident of Carleton near Skipton, born in 1849, Cecil Slingsby was best known for his Norwegian exploits. Married in 1882, his wife accompanied him to Norway in 1884 where she made the first female ascent of the Romsdalhorn.

He had started climbing in 1872 and the Fell and Rock Journal of 1929 described him as "a true Yorkshire dalesman, a good fellow, and a good goer". He published a book on Norway, and climbed in the Alps in 1892 with Mummery and Carr; in 1893 he made the first ascent of the Dent du Requin with Mummery, Collie and his Silsden friend Hastings. He also climbed extensively in the U.K. and explored the Dales both above and below ground. He was a Vice-President of the Alpine Club; Founder Member and President of the Climbers Club; an Original Member of the Fell and Rock; Hon Member of the Rucksack Club, the Yorkshire Ramblers and the Scottish Mountaineering Club; and a Fellow of the Royal Geographical Society. He introduced his son and daughter to mountaineering but sadly lost his son in the Great War. His daughter Eleanor (Len) continued to climb for many years, after she married Geoffrey Winthrop Young. Len was a close friend of the Wells sisters and a fellow member of the Pinnacle Club. The whole climbing community felt a great sense of loss with the passing of William Cecil Slingsby.

So the year ended, and for Trilby wells in particular, 1928 had been a very exciting year.

TRANSPORT TO THE MOUNTAINS

It might be prudent here to take stock of the distances travelled, and the time taken to travel those distances, in the period from the late Victorian era up to the late 1920s. Also the variety of methods of travel used, or indeed endured. This period saw two major improvements in transport: the expansion of the railway network and the development and improvement of roads and motor transport. Many mountaineers based in the south of England would travel by train to Windermere if going to the Lake District, or to Bangor or Llandudno Junction if visiting North Wales. From these stations, horse and cart, and later a few motorised vehicles, were available (sometimes after a long cold wait at the station) to take the climbers on to their destinations in places such as Ogwen or Langdale. Those going even further afield might walk over Sty Head to Wasdale, or Borrowdale, arriving in the early hours of the morning. Other stopping-off points included the west coast stations of present-day Cumbria, as well as Keswick.

In Wales, stations at Dolgellau, Barmouth and Porthmadog also gave access to the local hills and crags. Of course the repeat journey in the opposite direction was done a few days or a week later depending on the length of stay. E.H.Daniell of the Pinnacle Club wrote about walking up Cader Idris in 1913, presumably after travelling by train to the Barmouth area. She also mentioned that a week's holiday at a farmhouse near Ogwen could be had for £5, including a return train ticket from London! There were no buses initially in these remote areas, few cars and very few people. To travel to Pen-y-Pass, for Snowdon or Lliwedd, involved a long walk before attempting any summits or climbs. Bicycles, too, were often used, and again E.H.Daniell describes cycling from Porthmadog station to Pen-y-Gwryd and then on to Ogwen, before ascending Tryfan by the North Ridge- then cycling back to Porthmadog. Of course, a few of the more wealthy mountaineers soon became car owners (remember many of the early pioneers were professional people, some with well-paid jobs or their own business), and several owned motor-cycles too. The state of the roads at that time left much to be desired, yet the advent of motor transport increased greatly the accessibility of many parts of the Lake District and Wales.

Scotland, too, began to be opened up to more mountaineers as the railways pushed deeper and deeper into the Highlands and the west coast. The line to Fort William (5 hours from Glasgow) was opened in 1894; the line to the Kyle of Lochalsh in 1897, and to Mallaig in 1901. The use of sleeping cars and restaurant cars on these routes, as well as on lines in England, made the journeys much more pleasant and more comfortable. Linked to these lines were the ferries along Scotland's west coast, run by MacBrayne's from the 1880s. These all helped to make some of the Scottish islands more accessible, especially Skye and Arran.

So when we read of men and women walking and climbing in remote places like the Scottish Highlands or on the Isle of Skye, we should remember the arduous journey many had already undertaken to reach these destinations. It certainly wasn't easy for Trilby and Biddy Wells to travel from Ben Rhydding to Skye, Wasdale or Coniston, and they were fortunate that as professional people (both were teachers), they had the means and the holidays by which they could spend long weekends or weeks in the mountains. The Wells sisters were also fortunate that several of their friends in the Pinnacle Club owned motor-cars, and they would often be picked up from their Ben Rhydding home by friends en route to the mountains.

Blanche Eden-Smith, a friend of the Wells, owned a motor bike and sidecar and often carried fellow members to meets, some of these journeys being very notable for their speed and excitement! So when Trilby and Biddy Wells completed their exploits on Skye in the 1920s, we can imagine the outward and homeward journeys they undertook, using train, ferry and local vehicles to reach and return from Glenbrittle. They were following the precedents set by Mabel Barker and her fellow climbers, who wrote about cycling around Wasdale in 1906, and of journeying to Scotland in 1910.

We should also bear in mind the cost of accommodation and equipment at the time. Once again professional people could afford to stay at guest houses, hotels and farmhouse B and Bs, as well as having the means to purchase a rope, an axe, boots, clothing and a rucksack (and later on guidebooks to the climbs). Journeys to the Continent, to France, Italy, Switzerland and Norway for example, were not cheap and once again these mountaineers had the means and the time (often two or three months of holiday) to walk and climb in Europe. Paddy, Trilby and Biddy were good examples of this professional class.

1929 AND INTO THE 30s

At the start of 1929, Trilby, Biddy and Paddy Wells were able to attend the Pinnacle Club Annual Dinner in February (delayed from the previous autumn, and had an opportunity to discuss their 1928 exploits with other members who had equally exciting tales to relate. Biddy was also invited, as the representative of the Pinnacle Club, to the 21st Anniversary Dinner of the Ladies Scottish Climbing Club in Ballachulish, before attending the Pinnacle Club's Annual Meeting on March 30th in the Lakes.

Meets were held at several venues that year, and Trilby also attended an occasional Fell and Rock meet in the Lake District. Once again, a 1929 list of her fellow members of the FRCC reads like a "who's who" of climbing greats, including N.E.Odell, Haskett Smith, Bentley Beetham, Marco Pallis, George Seatree, George Basterfield and General Bruce. Also on the list of members were Paddy Hirst, Blanche Eden-Smith, Mabel Barker and Len Winthrop Young. The Wells sisters were certainly conversing with the pioneers of the 1920s.

In September, Trilby and Biddy organised a Yorkshire meet for the Pinnacle Club, at Almscliff Crag, near Otley. A committee meeting was held on the Saturday night, and members climbed for two days at Almscliff. Of particular note is the fact that Alison Adam joined this meet- her first Pinnacle meet; noteworthy because she was to organise an annual Yorkshire meet for many years to come, involving walking, climbing and pot-holing. Trilby attended many of these Yorkshire meets as she enjoyed them immensely. In later years she said she was so proud of her roots and liked to show others how beautiful the Dales were.

The 1930 Dinner was held in Manchester and meets were planned for the rest of that year. Mabel Barker led some first ascents in the Lake District and Blanche Eden-Smith (or G.) was active both in North Wales and the Lakes. Meanwhile, the Annual Meeting of the Pinnacle Club took place on April 19th at Torver, Coniston, where 'G' took over as secretary of the club, and Lilian Bray handed over the Presidency to Dr. Corbett. The Wells sisters attended some of the meets and of course the dinners and the annual meeting, but Biddy (now in her late 30s) and Trilby (early 40s) did not attend meets regularly.

Blanche Eden-Smith's diaries list her climbing days mainly in the Lakes up to Easter of 1930, but also mention the Pinnacle Club meet at Embsay, near Skipton on June 28th and 29th, organised by Marjorie Wood. Many routes were completed, and two good days were had. Though there is no mention of the Wells sisters in the diary entry for that weekend, it is fairly certain that Trilby and Biddy would have been present at a Pinnacle Club meet so close to their Ben Rhydding home as Trilby said later they always tried to attend meets held locally. Blanche followed up this meet with trips to Scotland and the Lakes. Paddy Wells was also active, making a visit to Scotland that year to climb some Munros with her husband John. They had climbed quite a few by this time and began earnestly "collecting" more and more of the Munros.

Trilby was present at the Langdale meet on the 1st November 1930, when she climbed with the Lakeland artist and guidebook illustrator W. Heaton Cooper, as well as Fell and Rock stalwarts Cain, Somervell and Alferoff.

In the 1930 Yorkshire Ramblers Journal there is a review of the latest Pinnacle Club Journal, and the article praises the ladies for their remarkable achievements since forming the club. In particular it mentions the traverse of the Cuillin Ridge by the three ladies, two of whom were of course Trilby and Biddy.

The following year 1931 saw an Easter meet for the Pinnacle Club at Buttermere followed by a Whitsun meet at Coniston. The Easter meet included ascents of several peaks including High Stile, Red Pike, Haystacks and Fleetwith Pike; Biddy Wells climbed Grassmoor Gully with Blanche Eden-Smith, and two days later no less than thirteen ladies scrambled on outcrops on Haystacks.

Coniston was the venue for the next meet at Whitsun, before another weekend at Wharncliffe Rocks. Later, Biddy and Trilby enjoyed another Yorkshire meet at Embsay Rocks near Skipton in June, climbing several routes each. Another Yorkshire meet attended by Trilby and Biddy Wells was on September 12th and 13th at Chapel-le-Dale, near Ingleton. It was this meet that saw the first Pinnacle Club group walk the "Three Peaks" of Yorkshire (Ingleborough, Whernside and Pen-y-Ghent). "G" describes the event in her diary as "fine, frosty weather, and added that the twelve-strong party visited Warcote Pot on the way back to their base.

The following month, yet another Yorkshire meet was held, again at Almscliff Crag. "G" stayed with the Wells sisters at Ben Rhydding and there were eight Pinnacle Club members present at the crag. Her diary lists the routes completed as Low Man Easy Way, Cup and Saucer, Leaf Climb, The Virgin, etc., but also includes a route known as "Hobby Horse". The next day Long Traverse, Long Chimney, Fluted Columns, etc. are listed, and "G" describes the weekend as "two days of lovely weather".

The final meet of 1931 was at Christmas, when the Pinnacle Club met at Kiln How, Rosthwaite, accompanied by "friends and relations of both sexes", according to Blanche's diary.

So into 1932 and an Easter meet at Capel Curig in Snowdonia. Once again, Blanche's diaries tell us of Biddy and Trilby Wells (listed as N. for Nellie and E. for Emily) climbing on Gashed Crag on Tryfan with Blanche. The weather was "fine, but bitterly cold strong wind. Had to abandon final chimney and traverse off, too cold!" They retreated to the valley and stopped off for tea at Gwern-y-Gof Uchaf, a local farmhouse. The next day, March 26th, Blanche explored the Devil's Kitchen area and went on to the Glyders in thick cloud, before the Annual meeting at night, with twenty-one members present. Two days later, Biddy and Blanche completed several "practice climbs" on the small crags behind the guest house they were staying in.

However, this Easter meet was very important in the history of the Pinnacle Club as this was when members spotted an old cottage at Cwm Dyli, near the foot of Snowdon, when they went to climb Lockwood's Chimney. After discussions with other members present it was agreed that they should find out who were the owners and whether it would be possible to rent the cottage as a club hut. After negotiations with the North Wales Power Company, the Pinnacle Club agreed a five-year lease, at ten pounds a year. The Club also paid a small fee for the installation of electricity and a few repairs to the cottage. All members agreed that the hut be known as The Emily Kelly Hut, in memory of one of the Pinnacle Club's founders, so tragically killed on Tryfan. Once again, Shirley Angell gives much detail about this in her excellent book about the Pinnacle Club.

In the meantime, while negotiations were taking place, Trilby and Biddy Wells attended a Fell and Rock meet at Coniston on April 23rd, again with "G". They walked up Tilberthwaite Ghyll and then back over the fells in rain and hail, and the following day the three ladies spent a bitterly cold day climbing on Dow Crags. So although not present at every meet, whenever they could attend, Trilby and Biddy were very active still.

The Emily Kelly Hut at Cwm Dyli.
Drawn by Alison Newey.
(Courtesy of the Pinnacle Club)

June 18th and 19th saw a Pinnacle Club meet at Embsay again, when members stayed at the Craven Heifer, Skipton. Seven members climbed several short gritstone routes at Embsay in good weather, and once again it is highly likely that Trilby and Biddy were there at yet another meet close to home.

September's Pinnacle Club meet was at the Moorcock inn at Hawes Junction in the Yorkshire Dales, with eight members present and a committee meeting held at night, again with "G" in attendance. This was followed by another meet at Almscliff Crag on October 15th and 16th, 1932. The party stayed at Ivy Cottage, North Rigton, just below the crag, and "G" records that eight members (which included Trilby and Biddy) climbed several routes over two days, finishing early at 2.30 p.m. on Sunday because of strong, cold winds. It was ever thus at Almscliff!

Then came the great occasion of the official opening of the Emily Kelly Hut. "G" described travelling to North Wales on November 4th, and then writes a paragraph in her diary describing the opening of the hut on November 5th, 1932. At 4.00 p.m. on that day the President, Dr. Corbett, officially opened the Emily Kelly Hut in the presence not only of members, but also invited guests who had supported the club since its foundation and during its early growth. Harry Kelly was of course a chief guest. Dr. Corbett made a short speech before everyone trooped inside for tea and cakes. It being November 5th, later in the evening, after many guests had departed, a bonfire blazed and fireworks were lit. A full account of the opening day is published in the Pinnacle Club Journal. "G" records 45 members present, some staying through to the eighth of November. There was also a mass ascent of Lockwood's Chimney- "as you do!" The three Wells sisters were present for the festivities; it was a landmark occasion in the annals of the Pinnacle Club, and when asked fifty years later about the day Trilby said she remembered that day quite vividly. She said it was a day for rejoicing, but also a sad day when thoughts of Emily Kelly came to mind. Trilby's Mont Blanc certificate hangs in the hut to this day.

To finish the year off, 35 members, including Trilby, Biddy and Paddy, attended the Pinnacle Club Annual Dinner at Capel Curig on December 30th and 31st. "G" notes in her diary that the dinner was delayed because of the late arrival of guests and speakers, but says it was still "a very good evening". However, the weather was too bad to go out on the hills for the next three days. Thus ended a very important year for the Pinnacle Club with the opening of their own hut. Incidentally, an excellent description of a typical weekend meet at the Cwm Dyli Hut was written by Evelyn Lowe and published in the Pinnacle Club Journal number 5, for 1932-34.

The new year of 1933 brought a first meet of the year at the Climbers' Hut at Parkgate, Coniston, and heavy snow affected the attendance. At Easter a meet was held at Burnthwaite, Wasdale, and again "G" met up with Biddy and Trilby Wells. They visited Pikes Crag but it was far too cold to climb, though they did manage a traverse of the Corridor Route to Styhead, and the two sisters did some scrambling on Lower Kern Knotts crag. Further meets took place that summer, but there is no record of any of the Wells sisters being there. A Skye meet also took place again without the Wells sisters, in October, and there was another Cwm Dyli meet in November. The Annual Dinner at Capel Curig, which the sisters did attend, on New Year's Eve, again completed the year of 1933.

Paddy meanwhile was making visits to Scotland with husband John to attempt yet more Munros. They had an ambition to climb not just the summits but all the 'tops' in the Munro tables as well. Each year the pair added to their list of ascents which would finally be completed in 1947. Throughout the 1930s, both Paddy and John Hirst used bicycles a lot, which they took on the train to Scotland and then were able to travel by bike to more remote mountains. Unfortunately we have no specific record of which peaks were ascended in each year.

Both Trilby and Biddy were by now very active on the committee of St. John's Church in Ben Rhydding and regularly attended meetings, organised social events, helped with the Sunday School and fund-raised for the Church. For Trilby in particular, involvement in the Church was to play a major role in her later life, as she was to become the local representative on the Bradford Diocesan Council in a few years' time.

Meanwhile, on the crags and mountains, many of the Wells sisters' friends and contemporaries continued to climb and walk all over the U.K. and Europe. One person of whom Trilby spoke very highly was Sid Cross, and his wife "Jammy" (Alice), and of their friendship over many years in the Lake District. Sid Cross climbed with H.M. Kelly up to 1938 and they formed quite a formidable partnership, climbing their last new route, The Rampart, on Scafell Shamrock in that year. Later, Sid and Jammy were to be prominent in Lakeland mountaineering history during their time at the Old Dungeon Ghyll Hotel in Langdale, and it was during that period that Trilby Wells came to know them so well. They also met when the Wells sisters attended the annual Fell and Rock dinners and meets. Their names are listed as being present at the dinners from 1926 through to 1934, and much later, along with Paddy's husband John Hirst. John and his friend Harry Spilsbury later teamed up to sing songs at the FRCC Dinners which were great social occasions. Trilby later mentioned how interesting it was to talk to people who had pioneered climbs in the U.K. and Europe, or who had been on Everest expeditions . Incidentally, in a photograph of the 1926 FRCC Annual Dinner at the Windermere Hydro, Trilby Wells appears front right on the picture.

To return to 1933, Blanche/"G"was on Skye in October and at a Pinnacle Club meet at Cwm Dyli in November. The Annual Pinnacle Club Dinner Meet was held at Capel Curig again on the 30th and 31st of December, and was attended by Trilby and Biddy Wells. Len Winthrop Young wrote an excellent article in the 1933 FRCC Journal about her early days spent with her father Cecil Slingsby at Carleton, near Skipton. She wrote of their early walks together in the local area and in the Dales, and of visits by famous mountaineers such as

Collie, Bruce, Haskett-Smith and Longstaff to her Carleton home, So too the Hopkinson brothers, C.E. Matthews and the Hastings brothers, as well as the female alpinist Lucy Walker. Geoffrey Winthrop Young was of course a regular visitor and eventually married Eleanor. Several Norwegians were also welcomed and were taken up Ingleborough or Pen-y-Ghent and even to Wasdale in mid-winter. She finished her article by saying how much her father loved the Yorkshire Dales and, in particular, the Craven hills nearer to home. Trilby, in one of her later interviews, spoke of her love of Wharfedale and how much "at home" she and her sisters felt when they returned to Ben Rhydding.

TOWARDS THE WAR

1934 began with a Pinnacle Club meet at the hut in Cwm Dyli in February and then an Easter meet at Coniston. This latter meet also included the A.G.M. on the evening of March 31st. A May meet was held again at Cwm Dyli, before Biddy and Trilby Wells attended the September meet at Buckden in Upper Wharfedale. This was a walking meet, and on Sunday September 16th the party completed a seventeen mile walk around upper Wharfedale. No doubt Trilby and Biddy were rather tired on returning to their teaching jobs the next morning at the Margaret Macmillan School in Bradford. All the time they were walking and climbing in the hills of the U.K., the pair were still working devotedly for the benefit of their pupils at the school.

Margaret Macmillan herself had been a great campaigner for improved conditions for children, particularly young children, in the 1890s and 1900s, and is associated with Bradford's pioneering contribution to child welfare and education. Both Trilby and her deputy Biddy held similar strong beliefs, and possessed a sense of dedication to their work.

Margaret Macmillan was born in 1860 in New York, and returned with her widowed Scottish mother to Inverness where her mother sadly died. Margaret was sent to be a governess in Edinburgh, and she and her sister Rachel became appalled at the conditions in which the poor children of the city lived. They both saw great inequality in society and became strong socialists. Both moved to London in 1888, and again were horrified by the living conditions of many families. In 1892 Margaret Macmillan met Dr. James Kerr, Bradford's School Medical Officer, who had completed the first medical inspection of elementary school children in Britain. This led to Margaret moving to Bradford in 1893, wanting to improve conditions for children in the city. The following year she worked alongside local Councillor Fred Jowett, influencing what happened in Bradford schools. Using her experiences, Margaret travelled all over the north of England to address meetings in public and in schools; in 1894 she joined Bradford's School Board. Thus began the educational work for which she became famous. In schools at that time there was no real physical nor pastoral care for children, especially the very young. Margaret Macmillan introduced school baths, improved ventilation in school buildings, and organised regular medical inspections and treatment, as well as helping to feed and clothe some children. This was quite innovative at the time and Trilby Wells and her sister were later to be equally innovative as they introduced similar ideas into their school.

In 1908, Margaret Macmillan moved to London again, where she continued her pioneering work in education, and wrote books on child welfare and education. She also opened clinics and schools in London before setting up a College to train teachers and nurses, all of whom were to empathise with Margaret's concerns for the plight of young children. Margaret Macmillan left an excellent legacy when she sadly passed away on March 29th 1931.

Her influence on Trilby and Biddy Wells was immense. Trilby felt the need to improve the welfare of not only the pupils in her own school, but also wanted to influence the other schools in Bradford who catered for young children. This was because Trilby saw some of the poor conditions in Bradford as she visited other schools. As a result, Trilby spent much time visiting the homes of children, suggesting ways in which parents could improve and help the health and development of their children. She also visited Children's

Homes and Orphanages, as well as other schools on a regular basis, often taking time off from her school and leaving Biddy in charge. Trilby was an organiser, a delegator, an inspirer and a dedicated hard worker, passing on her knowledge and ideas to teachers all over Bradford. On the crags, when climbing, Biddy Wells was usually the bold leader, Trilby a good second. A fellow member of the Pinnacle Club once wrote about this sisterly hierarchy, noting that the roles were reversed immediately they returned to the ground! So it was in their teaching careers; Trilby led from the front, supported at all times by her sister Biddy. Both of them were later to accompany the children when they were evacuated during the Second World War.

St. John's Church, Ben Rhydding, where Trilby and Biddy were members.

Trilby also continued to serve on the Church Committee in Ben Rhydding from 1934 to 1940, as well as furthering her occasional mountaineering experience alongside sister Biddy and sometimes her older sister Paddy. Trilby also attended meetings of the local Operatic Societies, sang at various events and organised excellent plays and sketches for the Church Social Committee. In addition, Trilby was a committee member of the Pinnacle Cub from 1931-34 and again from 1936-39. One wonders where she found the time and the energy to participate so fully in so many spheres.

So the mid 1930s was a busy time for both Trilby and Biddy Wells, and in 1935 they attended the Easter meet of the Fell and Rock at Wasdale. The 1935 FRCC Journal carried a review of the latest Pinnacle Club journal, describing it as a lively club of over eighty members, the Journal showing the club at its best. There was always a strong brother/sister bond between the two clubs and several women were members of both. The Fell and Rock had been super-supportive in 1921 during the formation of the Pinnacle Club. Meanwhile, the Pinnacle Club had held an early meet in February 1935 at Coniston, and members continued to climb throughout the year in Scotland, Wales and the Lakes. Of special note is Evelyn Lowe following Menlove Edwards (and others) up Longlands Route on "Cloggy"; and Brenda Ritchie put up the first female-led route on the same cliff in September. The year also saw the publication of Dorothy Pilley-Richards' excellent book "Climbing Days", still a classic in the twenty first century.

Unfortunately, this was also the year in which Geoffrey Winthrop Young took a bad fall while climbing on the Rothorn, an event which meant he never again returned to climb in the Alps. By all accounts he was lucky the fall was not fatal!

On a happier note, H.M.Kelly had begun editing the rock

climbing guides to the Lake District for the FRCC. These were the classic buff-coloured guides, the Second Series, which were printed between 1935 and 1938. They also contained illustrations by W. Heaton Cooper, who had earlier climbed with Biddy and Trilby in the Lakes. One of the authors of the guides was Sid Cross, a later close friend of the Wells sisters.

1936 saw Trilby return to the Pinnacle Club committee, and amongst other meets, she and Biddy organised a camping meet at Embsay, near Skipton, in June. The two sisters did all the planning and catering for seventeen members, who all climbed on Embsay and on nearby Eastby Crags over the weekend. At the end of that year (actually in early January 1937) the two sisters again attended the Pinnacle Club annual dinner at Capel Curig, and were joined by both sister Paddy and her husband John Hirst- quite a family gathering. The Hirsts were able to tell everyone about their exploits in Scotland in 1936, where they had added to their haul of Munros again. Also John described his trip to the Alps with his son John Hunter Hirst during the summer months.

1936 had also seen a great event in the Lake District. At Easter, W.P. Haskett-Smith had made the Jubilee ascent of the Napes Needle, to celebrate an ascent of fifty years previous. He had spent one day travelling by car from London to Wasdale; one day climbing on Pillar rock; and then arrived at noon on the third day, Easter Sunday, at the foot of the Needle. An estimated three hundred people had gathered at various viewpoints to watch this historic ascent, as, accompanied by Chorley and Speaker, Haskett-Smith reached the top of the Needle to cheers from all who were watching. Among the crowd were two sisters from Ben Rhydding, Trilby and Biddy Wells. An interesting account, and photograph, is published in the 1936/37 FRCC Journal. In the same Journal, H.M. Kelly writes about the history of climbing in the Lake District, and part of the article is devoted to the increase in women's participation in the sport of rock climbing. He even suggests that some women climbers are becoming as good as their male counterparts! It was of course Kelly's late wife Pat who instigated the setting up of the Pinnacle Club for women climbers in 1921.

During the 1930s, Trilby and Biddy also met a very famous mountaineer, John Menlove Edwards. In her interviews, Trilby mentioned that they had met him "in the thirties, I think, before the war", and that he appeared to be a "very strange man". Edwards, or Menlove as he was called by all and sundry, had qualified as a doctor in 1933 at Liverpool University and worked as a doctor in that city for several years. His specialism was psychiatry and mental health, but unfortunately his own mental health was beginning to decline in the 1930s, and it was no surprise that Trilby and Biddy formed their opinion of him. He was indeed a difficult man to know and to get along with, a future recluse, a homosexual (the phrase used at the time) and a loner. He was however a great and talented rock climber, with several first ascents in North Wales, and early ascents of difficult routes in the Lakes. He was also the author of four climbing guides and his life story is a fascinating read. He climbed with several well-known climbers, including Colin Kirkus, and also knew Geoffrey Winthrop Young and his wife Len. Menlove also climbed on occasions with Evelyn Lowe of the Pinnacle Club. When he met the two Wells sisters he was employed as psychiatrist to the Liverpool Child Guidance Clinic; this role was closely linked to Trilby's future work in Bradford. However, Trilby stated that Menlove was a man of few words, and was very difficult to engage in conversation.

In 1937 there were several Pinnacle Club meets, including at

Coniston in February and at Wasdale at Easter, where activities included climbing, walking and skiing. It was then that Trilby Wells came up with the idea for raising money for the Emily Kelly Hut at Cwm Dyli. Being the year of King George the sixth's Coronation, Trilby proposed a Coronation Hut Fund, to be used for repairs and improvements to the hut. This was agreed by all members and so the Hut Fund began. The Coronation took place in Whitsun week, a half-term holiday for the teaching Wells sisters, and a one week Pinnacle Club meet was held at the Cwm Dyli Hut. Biddy and Trilby showed they were still active by climbing on Lliwedd for a day, Biddy of course doing the leading. The Lliwedd guide book by J.M. Archer-Thompson had been printed in 1909 with about thirty seven routes described. By 1937 there were many more routes, and a new guidebook by Noyce and Edwards was to appear in 1939 just before the outbreak of the war. Much later, in 1972, Harold Drasdo produced the next volume. Guidebooks were still quite an innovation even in 1937, and in the 1920s there had been much discussion as to how much detail should be put into the guides. There were a few climbers who wanted very little information to be written down, leaving future climbers to find a sense of adventure and exploration on these routes. Others welcomed the description of routes, even of individual pitches. By 1937 there were guides to Lliwedd, Cwm Idwal and the Ogwen District, as well as Tryfan and Glyder Fach. In the Lake District, the famous Red Guides covering Great Langdale Area, Coniston Area, Pillar Area, Great Gable and Borrowdale, and finally the Scawfell Group, had been published in the 1920s, and other updated guides appeared in the 1930s. Scotland too had guide books to climbs on Ben Nevis and to the Isle of Skye; and several guides to Pennine gritstone crags had also appeared. So in 1937 it was possible to plan your meets ahead of the weekend by studying the guidebook to the area you wished to visit.

The 1937 Fell and Rock Dinner Meet was held at the Windermere Hydro on October 3rd, attended by all three Wells sisters. The following day a ceremony was held to celebrate the opening of the new FRCC hut at Brackenclose. Climbs were completed on Gimmer Crag and Dow Crag. Incidentally, the first treasurer for the hut was Harry Kelly, close friend of the sisters.

January 1st 1938 was the date for the Annual Dinner of the Pinnacle Club, again in Capel Curig, with thirty-five members present. John Hirst once again spoke as a guest, accompanied at the dinner by his wife Paddy and her two sisters. This dinner was held at the Bryn Tyrch Hotel, and was noteable for the appearance of Joyce Hirst, daughter of John and Paddy, on the weekend.

The main Easter meet was in Borrowdale, including the A.G.M. of the club. Trilby's Coronation Hut Fund had reached over seventeen pounds, and Trilby suggested at the meeting that a framed map of the Snowdon area be acquired, and hung at the Cwm Dyli hut in memory of Ruth Hale, a member tragically killed when climbing in Poland in 1937. At the same meeting it was agreed to try and extend the lease of the hut with the Power Company- this was successfully agreed later that year.

At the Easter meet, Biddy and Trilby were active on the crags, climbing Tophet Bastion on the Napes with Alison Adam and a new member Hester White. This was a route first climbed by Harry Kelly in July 1923, and is a 250 foot route of severe grade. The guide book lists seven pitches, but these can be joined together to make three or four longer pitches, which is what the ladies did. It is a classic Lakeland route, in a good position, and involves wall and crack climbing, a semi-hand traverse and a small pinnacle, before an easy exit up to the ridge. It is in no way an easy climb and once again demonstrates the climbing abilities of both sisters. The weather was excellent all week, with hot, dry days and cool nights. Trilby and Biddy had a great week of walking and climbing, before returning home to Ben Rhydding in time for the contrasting world of school teaching in Bradford on Monday morning.

The feeling in the country was now one of fear and expectation, as the problems in Europe caused by Hitler's rise to power began to suggest the possibility of war in Europe. Nevertheless, Whitsun saw Pinnacle Club members back in North Wales, and Mabel Barker was at the time walking the border between England and Scotland, an account of which is on page 218 of the 1939 Fell and Rock Journal. In the summer of 1938, club members were climbing in Skye, Wales, the Lakes and on Ben Nevis, as well as in Europe, Africa and the Far East.

The year ended with a Pinnacle Club dinner on December 31st, held at the Sun Hotel, Coniston, for a change, where walking and skiing were the main activities of those who attended. The new year of 1939 dawned and several meets were held by both the FRCC and the Pinnacle Club. The ladies met at the club hut at Easter and there were visits to the Alps in the summer months. John and Paddy Hirst apparently visited Scotland again, to climb a few more of the Munros on their list, no doubt feeling that the imminence of war might limit their opportunities in the near future. It seems strange to think that British mountaineers were still climbing in the French, Swiss and Italian Alps in August, just one month before war was declared in September 1939.

As war broke out, Trilby and Biddy Wells were working at the start of a new term at the Margaret Macmillan School. British cities were to become targets for German bomber raids and many schools were prepared for evacuation during the war years. This was soon to happen to the Wells sisters' school, though they were fortunate to be evacuated to a place near friends in Cheshire, as we shall see later.

THE SECOND WORLD WAR YEARS

The coming of World War Two caused climbing clubs to cancel most planned meets for the near future, though several ad-hoc meets were held in the Lakes and in Wales by men and women who were still keen to pursue their interests at any opportunity. Many women were signed up to work as ambulance staff, nurses, carers and A.R.P. Wardens, as well as for various voluntary organisations. Others worked in factories, on transport or on farms, doing many jobs formerly carried out by their male counterparts. Those women already in important or professional jobs mainly continued in their posts, including the three Wells sisters.

Trilby and Biddy Wells were unable to travel to the Lakes or North Wales in the autumn of 1939, and at the beginning of 1940 came another death in the Wells family. Jane Wells, widow of Cooper Wells and mother of Paddy, Trilby and Biddy, sadly passed away on February 18th, 1940 at the age of eighty-seven. Once again the family gathered at the tiny Church of Saint Helen at Denton, where interment took place in the grave where Jane's husband Cooper and daughter Mary were buried. John and Paddy Hirst accompanied Biddy and Trilby, and their brother Thomas from Bradford.

Though the service was held at Denton, the church at Ben Rhydding, Ilkley, had continued to play a big part in the lives of Biddy and Trilby, as they continued their work on committees, in the Sunday School and in organising social activities on midweek evenings. This was to temporarily halt, however, as in 1940 the Margaret Macmillan School was evacuated from Bradford to Cheshire, and along with the children went the two Wells sisters.

Now their great friend, Katie Corbett (or Dr. C.L. Corbett M.B. to give her a proper title), a founder member of the Pinnacle Club, was working in the Child Welfare Department of the Lancashire County Council, a job she held for thirty-two years. She lived in Cheshire, and the two Wells sisters were evacuated to a building close to where Dr. Corbett lived. This was of course great news for the Wells sisters, as they could keep in regular contact with her, and even managed to fit in a few walking days together. In later interviews, Trilby stated how important it was to keep up the contact between various Pinnacle Club members, either by occasional personal contact, by infrequent letters, and even on rare occasions, by telephone. In fact, a Pinnacle Club News Sheet was printed and sent out to all members in 1940, giving news updates and accounts of Alpine successes by club members during the previous year. There is also some ambiguity in the 1940 News Sheet, as, in the updated list of where members are working or living, it states that the two Wells sisters were evacuated to Nelson in Lancashire. Other sources suggest they were evacuated to Cheshire, near to Dr. Corbett. However, this evacuation was not to last the whole of the war, and both sisters were soon to return to their school in Bradford and to their home in Moorland View, Ben Rhydding.

In June of 1940, Trilby did manage to get away to the Lake District for a week during the half-term holiday, climbing for a few days in Wasdale and at Coniston with Dr. Corbett. They stayed at the Fell and Rock hut in Wasdale for a few days before moving to the Ship Inn at Coniston for the latter half of the week. There had been an official Pinnacle Club meet and an A.G.M. at Easter at the Cwm Dyli hut, and six more meets were tentatively planned for the next twelve months. Unfortunately, only one of these meets took place, there being travel restrictions and work duties intervening. However, several members did manage to visit the Cwm Dyli hut on a few occasions.

The Whitsun week in the Lakes remained in Trilby's memory for ever after a serious, yet hilarious, incident occurred on the last day of their stay. Trilby and Corbett walked through Grisedale Forest and accidentally entered Grisedale Farm property, somewhere which was restricted to all civilians, as it was a prisoner-of-war camp for captured German officers. The two ladies unwittingly marched out of the woods and straight through the camp, before suddenly being confronted by two armed soldiers, who demanded their identity papers. The ladies managed to convince the guards that they had made a genuine mistake, and were allowed to go on their way. However, when they arrived at the Ship Inn, the Police were waiting for them, and grilled the pair of them! The next day, they left for home, on the day that France fell to the German invasion. This was another tale to recount when they later met up with other club members at future meets.

1941 dawned and travel restrictions continued. However, Trilby and Biddy often found satisfaction in long weekend walks on Ilkley Moor and in Wharfedale. Members of the Pinnacle Club welcomed the occasional opportunity to visit the hut in Cwm Dyli, a place of peace and quiet amidst the activities of wartime Britain. Also, for those who could no longer visit the Alps, they could still climb in summer and winter on the crags of Snowdonia- some compensation at least. The Annual Meeting of the Club was held at Easter 1941, attended by Trilby Wells and a dozen others, Trilby acting as Chairman. The hut was host to a well–attended meet in August and again at the end of September. Trilby also managed to travel to the Lakes for the Fell and Rock Annual Meeting in Windermere and Langdale. She sat down to dinner with such noteables as Eustace

Thomas, Noel Odell (of Everest fame), Hargreaves, Macphee and several other leading mountaineers. At a time of travel restrictions, it is testament to Trilby's determination to keep up her mountaineering interests that she managed to attend these meets in 1941.

The following year, Trilby and Biddy Wells again were in the Lakes at Easter for the Pinnacle Club meet in Langdale from April 3rd to April 6th. Despite the afore-mentioned travel restrictions, about ten ladies arrived at the Old Dungeon Ghyll Hotel for the long weekend. The Wells sisters had made a "21st Anniversary Cake" for the occasion, and accompanied by several glasses of sherry, they also entertained the other ladies to humorous tales of past events in the Pinnacle Club. At this event, Biddy Wells was invited to become President of the Pinnacle Club, upon the completion of Mabel Jeffrey's three years in the role. While Biddy accepted that this was a great honour, she also said that she felt it would be better for Mabel Jeffrey to be re-elected as she had hardly seen any members (and there had been so few meets) during her three years as President. A thoughtful gesture from Biddy, and Mabel was swiftly re-elected.

Apart from climbing activities in 1942, Trilby and Biddy had now returned home from evacuation, and their school was once again functioning in Bradford. Trilby sat on the local Church Committee, ran the Church Social Guild with Biddy, helped out with the Sunday School and helped raise funds for the Church. Trilby also volunteered to represent the Church of St. John at the Diocesan meetings in Bradford. There had been other representatives from St. John's Church on the Diocesan Council before World War Two including some of Trilby's next door neighbours, and a Mr.G.A Collinson, also of Moorland View. They were replaced by Trilby Wells in 1942, when she also sat on the Church Vestry Committee and on the Parochial Church Council.

The work of the two sisters in Bradford also continued. Trilby was Head Teacher, Biddy her Deputy, and throughout the war their priority was the welfare of the children in their care. In her interviews later in her life, Trilby described the children as having "special needs", but added that in the 1940s those children at her school were described as E.S.N. (Educationally Sub-Normal), definitely not a phrase in use today. Trilby and Biddy introduced the children to a very wide and varied curriculum, with an emphasis on practical activities, a healthy lifestyle and cleanliness, together with the learning of domestic skills. It is not known in which year the visit to Mabel Barker's School at Friar Row had taken place, but again when interviewed in the 1980s, Trilby spoke of visiting Mabel at her school. There was obviously an effect on both sisters, who introduced several of Mabel Barker's ideas into their own curriculum. The sisters had first met Mabel at Almscliff Crag, and had also at the time climbed with Claude Frankland on a couple of occasions. Mabel had invited the Wells sisters to visit her school after she joined the Pinnacle Club in 1933 and had attended the Easter meet at Wasdale. Mabel's influence on activities at the Margaret Macmillan School is shown in the introduction into the curriculum of gardening skills (including growing vegetables for consuming at school), more physical education outdoors, the acquisition of art and craft skills (including outdoor sketching and painting), visits to local parks, woodlands and places of interest for "exploration", and the inclusion of "domestic subjects". Children were encouraged to wash and change clothes regularly, to wash body and hair regularly, to clean teeth, to eat good food and to generally look after themselves. Trilby later said that her hope was that these practices would be carried home by the children and would influence parents and siblings too. To add to this, Trilby often visited the homes of certain children to talk to the parents, as well as continuing to visit Orphanages and Children's Homes where some of her pupils lived. Again, she continued to visit other schools in Bradford to spread the idea of a more "inclusive" curriculum for all the children. Add to this Trilby's love of music, particularly Gilbert and Sullivan; Trilby even took her children to local concerts and to school music performances. Her involvement in the local and Bradford communities was to further increase after the end of the war. Once again, her able deputy, her "second", was sister Biddy- a reversal of their roles on the crags.

In 1943,there was no "official" Easter meet of the Pinnacle Club, (the first time this had happened), though members did occasionally manage to use the hut at Cwm Dyli for some walking and climbing. Mabel Barker had left the Lake District to take up a post in Peterborough where she remained until returning to Caldbeck on her retirement in 1946. Trilby Wells was a committee member of the Pinnacle Club from 1942-5 as she had been twice before, and was later to achieve higher office in the club. The year 1943 was apparently a blank year for the Wells sisters in terms of mountaineering, though their other interests and work no doubt kept them busy, and Trilby kept in touch with some of her closest friends in the club by letter. One notable article in the Fell and Rock Journal of 1943 was the obituary of Professor J. Norman Collie, born 1895, died 1942. He had climbed with Airedale climbers Slingsby and Hastings in the U.K. and in the Alps, describing them as "very happy occasions". Collie had explored and climbed extensively in Skye and in other Scottish areas, and had joined Mummery and Hastings in an audacious attempt on Nanga Parbat in the Himalayas in 1895. He was indeed a great mountaineer, and was yet another of those to whom the Wells sisters had chatted at F.R.C.C. dinners. Trilby was full of praise for the male members of the Fell and Rock, who had always been so supportive of women climbers and welcomed their membership and their presence at meets and social events.

So to 1944 and the war continued in Europe. John Hirst became President of the Rucksack Club, a great honour reflecting his long association with the club. Dorothy Pilley Richards was active in the United States where she lived with her climbing husband, and other women were active in the U.K. A Pinnacle Club Easter meet was held in Langdale, much to the relief of members who had communicated by letter for nearly two years. Fourteen members managed to attend the meet, climbing in decent weather for all three days. This was great for them as there had been so many restrictions on time and travel prior to this, and to actually begin climbing again was a tremendous relief.

The Pinnacle Club also agreed to subscribe to the Standing Advisory Committee on mountaineering, a forerunner of the British Mountaineering Council, now such an important organisation in the U.K. and indeed in world mountaineering. The Pinnacle Club also decided to produce a handbook. In other news, Len Winthrop Young joined the committee of the Ladies Alpine Club in that year, though it was once again a year of little mountaineering achievement. So too was the start of 1945, as war continued to change course in Europe and the rest of the world. Hopes for peace, and an end to hostilities, were high, but there was still only a small group, including Trilby Wells, who attended the Easter Annual Meeting of the Pinnacle Club at Cwm Dyli. Paddy and John Hirst meanwhile were able to visit Scotland occasionally throughout the war years. They were intent on ascending a few more Munros each year, and were anxious to complete the list when the war ended. This was soon to be achieved.

Victory in Europe came in May 1945 and Japan finally surrendered on August 15th of that year. Despite severe travel restrictions still in force, transport links still not fully functioning, petrol being scarce, food rations and people not being particularly well-off financially, mountaineers and climbers of both sexes began immediately to visit the mountains of the U.K. in increasing numbers. The Fell and Rock held their first Annual Dinner since 1938 at the Royal Oak Hotel, where H.M. Kelly was made an Honorary Member, and where once again John Hirst composed and sang some special songs for the dinner. Paddy was of course there to witness this honour, as were her two sisters. Travel restrictions did slowly begin to ease during the autumn of 1945, and Trilby said that she and Biddy travelled to climb in both the Lakes and North Wales that autumn.

Back in Bradford, the fourth of July saw a special occasion for the schools of the city. It is recorded in the School Logbook that Trilby Wells "took a party of 13 children to the Schools Musical Festival of Thanksgiving and Dedication at Easterbrook Hall", to celebrate victory in Europe. Other entries in the logbook show Trilby visiting local schools to attend classes and concerts during 1944 and 1945, as often as once a month. She particularly visited Cottingley Manor School on a regular basis. In July 1945, she visited Council Stores at Southfield Lane to inspect stock and to make new recommendations to Bradford Education Committee about what was needed in the city schools. Thus, Trilby's work and influence in Bradford continued. The Margaret Macmillan School was also visited in July 1945, by both the Director of Education for Bradford, and by His Majesty's Inspectors of Schools, who had heard of the school's growing reputation and pioneering work in extending the curriculum for special needs children. Then, in September 1945, as war had ended in Europe and in the far east, Trilby and Biddy organised a "Victory Party" at the school for 110 children, with food and drink, party games and a conjuror to entertain the pupils and staff. Trilby later spoke of her appreciation of the staff; she held them in such high esteem at the Margaret Macmillan School.

In October 1945, Trilby attended a meeting of the Schools Horticultural Society at the Town Hall, with the idea of establishing an exhibition or show whereby Bradford pupils could demonstrate their gardening and horticultural skills, with fruit, flowers and vegetables. A year later this was to happen! At her school, children were being visited by local craftsmen, including carpenters, weavers and cobblers, to show the children some of the skills they needed to procure jobs after leaving school. This was certainly an innovation in schools at the time. On a personal note, the Logbook also states that twice in the autumn of 1945, Miss Wells was absent for two days with a "severe cold"!

In 1946, climbers were again active in the U.K. More club huts were opening and the Pinnacle Club had reciprocal rights of access to some of these huts in North Wales and the Lake District. The Easter meet of 1946 was held at the new Fell and Rock hut in Langdale, at Rawhead, where the first hut warden was Sid Cross, later to run the Old Dungeon Ghyll Hotel as proprietor, and a friend of the Wells sisters. Several new members joined the Pinnacle Club; the Fell and Rock increased its membership and resources; John H. Hirst, son of Paddy and John, became Treasurer of the Rucksack Club for the next fourteen years; the Queen visited Snowdonia (and the Pen-y-Gwryd Hotel) to celebrate the proposed formation of the National park; a Pinnacle Club meet was held at Lagangarbh in Scotland; and a large Pinnacle Club meet took place in November at the Black Bull, Coniston.

Harry Kelly was still taking charge of the Fell and Rock climbing guidebooks and in 1946 was recruiting climbers to help update these guides to the Lakes. He recruited men like Peascod, Dolphin,

A.T. Hargreaves, Bentley Beetham and Sid Cross, and Kelly himself continued as editor of this Third Series (though they were mysteriously labelled “2nd Series”!!). This editorial work continued until the late 1960s.

At the same time, Geoffrey Winthrop Young became the first President of the newly-formed British Mountaineering Council from 1945 to 1947. This coincided with a brand new publication “Climbing in Britain”, published by Penguin Books at a cost of one shilling (5p), and edited by J.E.Q. Barford of the Climbers’ Club. Young had set up a conference in 1944 at the Alpine Club in London, to establish a mountaineering council. He had a great national influence on mountaineering as President of the Alpine Club (1941-3), as an experienced alpinist and an accomplished author. Young saw the need for a unification of all aspects of mountaineering in Britain and also the need for mountain training schemes. Distinguished mountaineer Jack Longland was also a keen supporter. Thus the B.M.C. came into being. With the success and high number of sales of “Climbing in Britain”, a house journal was now planned, and the first edition of “Mountaineering” was to appear in 1947.

New routes had been put up throughout the war in Scotland by such as B.P. Kellett and J.H.B. Bell on Ben Nevis and within two years of the war finishing thirty eight new routes were created in Glencoe by people such as John Cunningham and Bill Murray. The Peak District gritstone areas saw a great increase in the number of routes after 1945, as did Borrowdale and other Lake District areas. Beetham, Peascod, Birkett and Dolphin were among the leaders of this Lake District development.

At the same time, Trilby and Biddy Wells were as active as ever in all walks of life. During 1945-6 Trilby visited Odsal House, Great Horton Primary, Green Lane School and several other establishments in Bradford, even acting as temporary Headteacher at Odsal House for a week or so, leaving Biddy (named as Miss Sarah Ellen Wells) in charge at Margaret Macmillan School in 1946. Some of Trilby's visits were in the company of Educational Psychologists, and jointly they were assessing children's abilities and educational needs. Sometimes too, in midweek Trilby would attend the Juvenile Court in Bradford, where certain young pupils of whom she had knowledge were appearing; she would often speak up on their behalf. In November 1946, Trilby again left Biddy in charge at Margaret Macmillan School for a few days, as she attended a national conference on "Mental Health and Education" in London. The following spring, she spent several days at Bradford Central Clinic, "testing children". As previously noted, Trilby and Biddy Wells were aware of the need for children's education to include their physical, emotional and mental health, as well as their academic progress and skills acquisition. College students often visited the Macmillan School to observe lessons and activities, and to discuss with Trilby Wells her philosophy for educating the whole person. Trilby also found time to attend committee meetings of the Schools Horticultural Society and to organise shows of produce. Along with her teaching work, her church commitments and her mountaineering exploits, it is quite amazing how much energy she must have possessed during this period.

Climbing was still high on the list of activities for Trilby and Biddy. In 1946 they again met members of the Fell and Rock and Pinnacle Clubs and attended several meets. By the beginning of 1947 they were keen to visit Scotland again as their previous visits had all been pre-war. Both sisters missed the annual Easter meet at Cwm Dyli, but at Whitsun it was time to visit Skye again. In her later interviews, Trilby Wells almost waxed lyrical about the "beautiful

Isle of Skye", saying that despite very mixed weather whenever they visited the isle, the dramatic scenery was one of her favourite sights in her lifetime. Her eyesight was fading in the 1980s and she doubted she would be able to appreciate the views if she had visited in later life. "I have my fond memories though" she added.

The Skye meet was a joint one with the M.A.M. (the Midland Association of Mountaineers) and climbs were completed on the Cioch (Direct and West Climbs) and on Sron-nc-Ciche (Mallory's Slab and Groove). They also visited the Inaccessible Pinnacle, the ridge from Sgurr Alasdair to Sgurr Dearg, and generally had a great week exploring the Dubhs and the main peaks. Remembering that Trilby Wells was now 58 years old and Biddy Wells 53 (and most of their companions were of similar age), it is remarkable the level of fitness and commitment these ladies possessed.

Elder sister Paddy Wells was also in Scotland over the Whitsun week, trying to complete her list of 543 Munro tops. She and husband John had been working through the list of mountains and tops since the mid 1920s and this passion had meant that holidays at New Year, Easter, Whitsun and summer had often been devoted to completing the list. Paddy wrote an interesting article in the Pinnacle Club Journal number 7 describing her achievement. At first they simply climbed the peaks, but after meeting a S.M.C. member who was just completing the Munros, Paddy and John realised just how many they had already climbed. Their plan was hatched! Paddy decided that they would leave Ben More, on the Isle of Mull, as the last "peak" to be ascended; and so, on May 28th, 1947 they topped Ben More, before completing the "tops" in August 1947 by climbing Ben Dearg, near Ben Nevis. In the official list of "Compleaters" (sic) of the Munros, number 9 on the list is J. Hirst; and number 10 on the list is Mrs. J. Hirst. So only eight other people before them had officially completed the list since its inception in 1891, and they were thought to be the first married couple ever to achieve the feat. They were called "the Southport-based Hirsts" in the lists, and Paddy has been described as "possibly an even more accomplished hillgoer than her husband"! She was of course vastly experienced and had been the second President of the Pinnacle Club in the 1920s. Also, many of the Munros had been climbed under winter conditions, again showing the high capabilities of Paddy Wells.

So 1947 was an enjoyable Scottish year for all three sisters. Paddy returned to her Southport home, while Trilby and Biddy were soon back at Moorland View, Ben Rhydding, where they continued to be active in their church commitments. A Parish Church Newsletter of January 1945 describes a meeting of the Church Social Guild: "The Misses Wells brought the house down with their topical sketch and the screaming play which they produced entitled 'Acid Drop', with which the evening closed" In July 1945, the Misses Wells were praised for their dedication to rehearsals and the making of costumes for the Sunday School Festival. In December of that year, with demobilisation increasing, Trilby and Biddy were involved in welcoming back to the church many men from the forces. Their hard work was to continue in 1946 when three one-act plays were produced by the sisters in January, called "Bloaters", "Behind the Bathroom Door" and "Shocks in a Parish"- all "well-performed and received". Evening social events that year included quizzes, handicrafts, any questions, games, talks, whist drives, discussion groups and tennis sessions- all organised by Trilby and Biddy Wells. Again in 1947 the sisters are mentioned in their Church Newsletter as "the Misses Wells brought the evening to a close with a topical sketch of their own which was both clever and amusing" Added to this, both sisters were generous in providing gifts and raffle prizes, to raise funds for the Church. Trilby also served on the Church Council from 1947 through to 1961. Just where did they get their energy?

The dramatic presentations, songs and sketches reflected the sisters' love of theatre and especially of Gilbert and Sullivan. On many climbing trips, evenings at the huts were often spent in members taking turns to "perform", and foremost amongst the performers were Trilby and Biddy. Harry Kelly and other climbers were also great fans of Gilbert and Sullivan; and John Hirst and Harry Spilsbury, who always performed at Fell and Rock events, based many of their songs on tunes from Gilbert and Sullivan works.

In mountaineering terms, 1947 ended for the pinnacle Club with a Yorkshire Meet in October and a wet weekend at Cwm Dyli in December. Meanwhile, Arthur Dolphin was climbing new routes in the Lake District, seconded by another Ilkley climber Des Birch. On 23rd June 1947 they climbed two new routes at Raven Crag, Walthwaite, called 'Proteus' and 'Deuterus', both at V.S. grade. Des Birch was to climb on many occasions with Dolphin, and is mentioned in the excellent book "Memories of Dolphin". Des was a formidable athlete and had represented England on the athletics track. He was to become one of the three men who initiated the Three Peaks Run around the Yorkshire peaks of Pen-y-Ghent, Whernside and Ingleborough. He was well known as a teacher at Ilkley Grammar School and was a very experienced caver and pot-holer.

Finally for 1947, Trilby and Biddy held a tea party at their school, decorated for the occasion, on 29th November, for the children to celebrate the Royal wedding of Princess Elizabeth (Queen Elizabeth the second) and Prince Philip, which took place the next day. November 30th was a national holiday for the wedding, and Trilby and Biddy had a welcome day off.

TRILBY'S PRESIDENCY

1948 began with Paddy and John Hirst travelling yet again to Scotland. Despite their completion of the Munros the previous year, they had fallen in love with the beauty and remoteness of the Highlands and Islands, and continued to explore new and remoter areas, as well as repeating the ascents of several peaks and climbs. They also continued their habit of taking bicycles on the train and cycling to out-of-the-way places. Trilby and Biddy Wells also remained active, in mountaineering, education and church matters.

Trilby continued to serve on various church committees; she and Biddy organised social events at St. John's; Trilby once again visited other Bradford schools; and they both managed to snatch weekend or holiday trips to the mountains. Sometimes these were local visits to Wharfedale crags or into the Dales, but they also managed occasional visits to North Wales and the Lake District. On January 3rd-5th, 1948, the Pinnacle Club held its first "Post-War Dinner Meet" at Coniston, where Dr. T.H. Somervell was the guest speaker, and climbing took place on Dow Crag. The Easter meet was held at Cwm Dyli, along with the A.G.M., and six new members joined. Whitsun saw Pinnacle Club members in Scotland with the Ladies Scottish Mountaineering Club, at Glencoe, whilst the August meet was held at Cwm Dyli. The Yorkshire meet in October saw Trilby and Biddy Wells, along with Bray, Corbett and others, on a twenty mile walk exploring Malham and Gordale Scar, before a second day in Upper Wharfedale near Kettlewell.

In the meantime, at Margaret Macmillan School, three of His Majesty's Inspectors of Schools had arranged another visit for

August 4th, 1948 and both sisters had been preparing hard for this inspection. The H.M.I. Report was very positive about both the pupils and the staff: "The work being done by the Headmistress and her staff is having a valuable ameliorative effect upon the lives of these handicapped children" concluded the report. "The Headmistress and her staff give devoted service to the school". The report particularly mentioned the positive effects of gardening, physical education, arts and crafts, handicrafts and domestic subjects, preparing pupils for life after schooldays. Notice the phrase "effect upon the lives" and not just an effect on their classroom education. Trilby and Biddy Wells were delighted with the results of the inspection!

After the summer holidays, Trilby continued to entertain visitors from other schools and even occasionally from other parts of the country, come to study the methods and curriculum of the school. College students also visited regularly. In November the school held a huge bonfire party on the fifth, for which the boys built the fire, the girls made the guy, all pupils made the refreshments, and parents, siblings and friends were invited to attend. This was another example of Trilby's idea of opening up the school to families, to colleagues from education, and to the wider community. Indeed, there were several 'Open Days' during Trilby and Biddy's time at Margaret Macmillan School.

Also in 1948, a meeting at the Connaught Rooms in Bradford in November led to the setting up of the Bradford Gilbert and Sullivan Society. Trilby was by this time singing with the Menston Amateur Operatic Society, and her first production was called "Patience". The Bradford G.and S. Society would hold its first production, "The Gondoliers", in June 1950, at the Elite Picture House in Bradford, and subsequent productions were held at the Alhambra Theatre. Over 200 members joined the Society in the first three months, over

120 of them 'acting' members, and the membership swelled to over 300 within a year. This reflects the immense popularity of Gilbert and Sullivan at the time. The Menston Society rehearsed in Menston but shows were put on in Ilkley. Trilby Wells remained a member for twenty years, and remained a patron of the Bradford G. and S. Society until her death in the 1980s.

1948 also saw the first ever visit to Arran by Trilby and Biddy Wells. They had long been anxious to visit the island wishing to compare it to their favourite, Skye. They took the last bus from Ilkley to Leeds at 11.00 p.m. and boarded the 2.00 a.m. train to Kilmarnock; from there a local train took them to Ardrossan for the ferry, after a hearty breakfast in the town. At Brodick, on Arran, they met John and Paddy Hirst, and Lilian Bray. After lunch they took a bus tour of the island and were very impressed, despite Trilby falling asleep during the bus trip! They visited Glen Sannox in sweltering heat and scrambled, paddled and sunbathed. They then climbed Binnein and Goat Fell the next day, before visiting Glen Rosa later in the week. Bray, Paddy and Trilby also climbed Chliabhain while Biddy and John Hirst went up the A'Chir ridge and on to Cir Mhor. They had a wonderful week and promised to return again soon. Leaving by the 7.00 a.m. bus, they returned to Ben Rhydding in time for tea. In a later article, Trilby describes the week as "not very energetic"!

January 1949 saw the first Annual Dinner Meet that the Wells sisters could not attend (we know no reason why), but a distinctive honour was soon to come Trilby's way. The Easter General Meeting marked the end of Evelyn Leach's Presidency, and the committee members had for weeks been trying to persuade Biddy or Trilby Wells to take over the mantle of President. Both of them refused! However Lilian Bray was persistent, and eventually persuaded Trilby to accept the invitation. She was duly elected at the A.G.M as President of the Pinnacle Club for the period 1949-52. When recalling this honour in her later interviews, Trilby much preferred to talk about the meets and the hut at Cwm Dyli. She talked about how wonderful Lliwedd was as a crag, so close to and accessible from the club hut, and loved by all the members. She also spoke about her days and evenings at Almscliff Crag, "our climbing and picnics, looking out over lower Wharfedale". She was nevertheless very proud of her time as President.

Trilby Wells, President, The Pinnacle Club, 1949-52.

Another item which made Trilby Wells quite animated was when she talked about "wet meets". In Wasdale, there was always the occasional visit to the Y Boulder in Mosedale when the upper fells were too wet or hidden in cloud; but the highlight in wet weather was the "fun and friendship when sitting and chatting in the huts". "The kettle was always on" she added, and members always had tales to tell. These were often long, rambling and hilarious, and Trilby added that though many were true, "certain members could make up the most incredible of stories", much to their colleagues' amusement. "It kept us amused for hours and kept our minds off the rain outside the window". Trilby, Biddy and others would often change the words of a Gilbert and Sullivan piece in order to make the song relevant to some recent club event or escapade. As bashful as ever when talking about her achievements, Trilby said: "I didn't want to be President- my sister Biddy pushed me into it really" Of note is that at her inauguration as President, Gwen Moffatt, renowned author and mountaineer, was a guest and joined the Pinnacle Club that weekend.

The year of 1949 saw three important events. There was a Pinnacle Club Meet in August based near Zermatt which was a very successful and happy occasion, but the death of member E.H.Daniell (the novelist E.H.Young) brought a great sadness to her fellow members. Born in 1911, she had been a member for many years, and her executors left a gift of her books to the Pinnacle Club. The third event of the year was also a tragic death, when popular member Freda Rylatt slipped and fell off Flying Buttress, a climb on Dinas Cromlech in Llanberis Pass, on October 30th. Freda was described in the Club Journal as "a fine climber, a great companion and a true friend". Freda's climbing gear was donated to the club, and a subscription fund in her memory enabled the club to purchase new comfortable mattresses for the Cwm Dyli hut.

On a brighter note, one event involving the Wells sisters was a further visit to Arran in 1949, again at Whitsun. Although only five members took part, four were original members of the Pinnacle Club. Unfortunately, the weather was not kind to them for the first half of the week and they failed to reach the windy summit of Goat Fell. The next day they visited Tarbet by steamer and went walking. On the Wednesday they climbed Cir Mhor in slightly better weather, followed by a trip to Holy Island the next day. On Friday they had a bus tour of the island, before Biddy and Trilby set off for home. Their journey home was marred by British Railways: "No morning coffee or lunch! All we had to exist on were three chocolate biscuits and a thermos full of tea!"

Towards the end of the year, the death was reported of George Basterfield on November 13th, a former President of the Fell and Rock; he had been an active mountaineer and climber, who had also produced a book of poetry and prose called "Mountain Lure" He was of course well-known to the Wells sisters. The 1949 Fell and Rock Dinner paid tribute to him. It was held at the Royal Oak, and Trilby, Biddy and Paddy all attended. John Hirst and his great companion Harry Spilsbury once again sang their after-dinner songs. Thus ended the first calendar year of Trilby's Presidency.

The next year started as the old year finished, with yet another dinner! This was the 1950 Annual Dinner Meet of the Pinnacle Club at the Black Bull, Coniston, over New Year's Eve. The arrangements were made by Trilby and her able deputy Biddy, including the fun and games on New Year's Eve, and members (including the Wells sisters) climbed on nearby Dow Crag. Next came the Easter meet, at one of Trilby's favourite venues, Middle Row, in Wasdale. Both sisters enjoyed the weekend, walking with Bray and Corbett on Scafell and Scafell Pike. Trilby chaired the Annual Meeting on the

Saturday night.

The Whitsun meet was held at Cwm Dyli, as was the August meet, the Whitsun one being a joint meet with the Ladies Scottish Climbing Club. In September Biddy joined John Hirst and a few Pinnacle members at Arncliffe in the Dales for a weekend meet.

THE PINNACLE CLUB

1921—1951

President :
Miss E. WELLS,
Westmead, Moorland View, Ben Rhydding, Yorks.

Vice-President :
Mrs. E. W. LEECH,
79, Pownall St., Macclesfield, Ches.

Hon. Secretary :
Miss M. WOOD,
1, Grove Avenue, Frizinghall, Bradford.

Hon. Treasurer :
Miss K. W. H JACKSON,
66 Roslyn Gardens, Gidea Park, Romford, Essex.

Hon. Librarian :
Miss E. M. PYATT.

Hon. Editor :
Mrs. H. C. BRYAN.

Committee :
Dr. C. L. CORBETT — Miss P. RAVEN
Miss E. PYATT — Miss P. WILD
Miss A. WILSON — Miss C. COOPER

Hon. Hut Secretary and Treasurer :
Miss J. TAYLOR

Hon. Auditors :
Miss L. LAMBRICK — Miss H. A. TURNER

The first page of a Pinnacle Club Booklet, issued in 1951,
showing Trilby Wells as President.
(Courtesy of the Pinnacle Club)

The final meet of the year was planned for New Year's Eve at Coniston, and John Hirst was to be the guest speaker, but he and Paddy were unable to travel to the Lakes because of heavy snow. Despite the snow across the north of England, Trilby and Biddy were able to reach Coniston, and organised party games after the meal. Snow on the hills was very wet and soft so most people kept to low-level walks near Tarn Hows. This was a period in their lives when both Wells sisters were reverting to their 'early days' of mountaineering, doing just a little rock climbing but plenty of mountain walking. Paddy, too, had been in Scotland again, walking and scrambling with husband John and though now 66 years old, she was apparently still quite fit and active.

The Pinnacle Club produced a Journal in 1950. This was a momentous publication as the previous Journal had been the 1938 version. In her foreword to the Journal, Trilby (writing as E. Wells) wrote of how the war years had restricted finance and opportunity to publish a Journal, and of her great satisfaction in finally presenting to members a new publication. The club had languished during the war years, yet members had managed to snatch a few days here and there- a climb or two- a breath of mountain air- a hut weekend. "All these things helped us to hold on to the things that really endure". She wrote of how the club revived after the war, the pleasure of reunions at dinners and meets, and the pleasure of seeing new members join. She ended by writing: "May this journal be the forerunner of many!" Also in the Journal was an excellent article describing Trilby's two visits to Arran, and a wonderful photograph of Trilby Wells, President 1949-52 as a frontispiece. Trilby questioned in her Arran article whether Arran would be as beautiful as "our first love, Skye. Even now", she writes, "after a second visit, I cannot make up my mind; Skye can be so wild and so forbidding, while Arran is more gentle, more alluring. It has so much variety packed into so small a compass. Where else can one find mountains, hills, countryside and sea coast all in one small island?" Trilby does not answer her own question, though in later life she extolled the virtues of Skye and said it was always a favourite place for her and Biddy.

The following year began with a very wet Pinnacle Club meet at Edale. At an earlier committee meeting the club had agreed to stock up the library with all the new climbing guides, and these would soon be used at the Whitsun meet at the Old Dungeon Ghyll in Langdale. It had recently been taken over by Sid and Jammy Cross. This was the real start of a long and happy friendship between Sid and Jammy and the Pinnacle Club members. Mind you, anyone who met the pair almost always became friends, as they were renowned for their pleasantness and their hospitality. The Wells sisters had known Sid and Jammy for several years prior to this, and had climbed with them on occasion.

September saw yet another Yorkshire meet, attended by Trilby and Biddy Wells, this time at Austwick, near Ingleborough, in fine weather, followed by a wet weekend in November at the Cwm Dyli hut. Later, the Annual Dinner followed, with a Presidential speech by Trilby. 1951 sadly saw the death of one of the truly great pioneers of British mountaineering, Ashley P. Abraham, who passed away on October 9th. He was of course the first President of "The Fell and Rock Climbing Club of the English Lake District" (to give it its full title). He and his brother George climbed with Owen Glynne Jones in their early lives and were as famous for their photographic exploits on the crags as they were for their first ascents of climbs. From late Victorian times, the brothers explored the Lake District, climbing gullies, ghylls and ridges. In 1895 they went to Skye for the first of many visits, producing a wonderful book, "Rock Climbing in Skye", with a map of The Cuillins and several illustrations. They continued to climb first ascents in the Lakes and in North Wales, as well as visiting the Alps and the Dolomites. Ashley remained a club member all his life and his obituary appeared in the 1952 F.R.C.C. Journal. On the next page was another obituary, written by Sid Cross, of A.T. Hargreaves, another Lakeland pioneer. Two mountaineers that the Wells sisters had met many times.

The Fell and Rock Annual Dinner that year was held at the Old Dungeon Ghyll Hotel, under the guidance of Sid and Jammy, where John Hirst and Harry Spilsbury once again sang their new songs, accompanied by Mrs. Spilsbury on the piano. The song "Annual General Meeting" was reproduced in the 1952 Fell and Rock Journal. Paddy accompanied her husband and her two sisters, Trilby and Biddy, to the Dinner.

Finally for 1951, the Pinnacle Club produced a small booklet to celebrate thirty years of the club. It contained a list of officers of the club and the rules; a list of members and their addresses (and who was an Original Member); lists of past and future meets and who attended; details of the club hut and of reciprocal rights to several other huts; general information about meetings and the new British Mountaineering Council; finances of the club; and details of the club library. On the front page was the title: President: Miss E. Wells, West Mead, Moorland View, Ben Rhydding, Ilkley.

1952 was to see the end of that Presidency. Trilby and Biddy had been to the Lakes a couple of times notably for the Fell and Rock Dinner (they missed very few of these!), during the winter months, and also for the Pinnacle Club Meet at Coniston at Easter. Trilby stood down as President, to be replaced by Nea Morin, another well-known and very accomplished climber, famous for the route in the Llanberis pass which bears her name. Nea Morin was also an excellent alpinist who brought a great knowledge and experience to the club in all her years of membership and office. This year was perhaps a sign of a change in the Pinnacle Club as some of the younger, and better, climbers began to take office, and harder and harder climbs were being led by members. There was certainly a general expansion of women's climbing during these next decades.

While the Wells sisters were visiting Wales and the Lake District, and some members visiting Scotland, it must be remembered that petrol was still rationed and not everyone had a car or motorcycle. Trains and buses were well used, and there are tales of climbers arriving at Bangor station late at night, to then travel in a battered old charabanc up to Ogwen and Capel Curig. Many then walked on to other venues. So access to the mountains and the climbs was still not easy.

There were several visits to the Pinnacle Club Hut during the year, and a large club meet there in August, followed by a Yorkshire Meet in September. Here they held a committee meeting involving Trilby, Biddy, Dr. Corbett and Marjorie Wood, as Trilby was still a Vice President until 1955. They discussed the venue for the annual dinner, which was eventually postponed until February 1953. Trilby then joined sister Paddy and her husband John at the Fell and Rock Dinner (but not Biddy for some reason) in the Lakes. It is interesting to note that when the attendance lists were signed, Paddy wrote her name as "Annie" Hirst, and Trilby signed as "Emily" Wells.

A footnote to the end of 1952 regards two other Ilkley climbers. On September 14th, climber Des Birch and his fiancée (later his wife) Jean Lovell, made the first ascent of Mare's Nest Buttress on Pike's Crag, in the Lake District, a 250 foot climb of Severe standard. Both were to continue climbing for many more years.

TOWARDS RETIREMENT

1953 was to be Trilby's final year at the helm of the Margaret Macmillan School in Bradford, but she remained as devoted as ever to her school and to her children. Her usual activities continued around Bradford and lots more visitors and students came to her school. Trilby also continued to work for the Church in Ben Rhydding, serving on the Church Council from 1947 through to the 1960s. Trilby is mentioned in lots of minutes of meetings, proposing and seconding items, fund raising, arranging social activities and serving on the finance committee. It was about this time that Trilby Wells was elected as a representative to the Diocesan Council Conference in Bradford, along with another resident of Ben Rhydding, a Mr. Farrar. She also remained active in the local Amateur Operatic Society and the Bradford Gilbert and Sullivan Society.

So too in the Pinnacle Club. She and Biddy attended meets in 1953 and took part in the Annual Dinner (postponed from 1952) at the Old Dungeon Ghyll Hotel in Langdale in February. Paddy Hirst also attended, and once again John Hirst sang songs after the dinner. The next day they climbed on Pavey Ark and Bowfell Buttress. Later, Paddy and John visited Scotland again at Easter.

This was of course the year of the first ascent of Everest on June 29th. Several members of the successful expedition were later to attend various club dinners and all three Wells sisters were fortunate to meet and talk with them at these dinners. The summer ,however, also brought sad news for Yorkshire and Lake District climbers, as on July 25th, 1953, the great climber Arthur Rhodes Dolphin was killed while descending from the Dent du Geant, when, unroped from his Belgian climbing partner, he slipped on ice and fell to his death. He was an excellent climber, famous for his ascent of Kipling Groove on Gimmer Crag (so called because he found it "ruddy 'ard"), but also for many other first ascents. He made Almscliff Crag his home crag at first before progressing to the Lake District crags, where he was already leading on Dow Crag by the age of fourteen. After climbing in North Wales and the Lakes, he graduated to Alpine routes, including the Zmutt Ridge on the Matterhorn, the Grepon and many classics around Zermatt and Chamonix. His obituary in the 1953 Fell and Rock Journal was written by John Cook, who, along with Ilkley climber Des Birch, had climbed regularly with Arthur Dolphin on Yorkshire gritstone and in the Lakes. He was a very popular man and would be sadly missed by the climbing fraternity.

The year ended with a Fell and Rock Club Dinner at the Royal Oak, attended by John Hunt and Alfred Gregory (from the recent Everest expedition) and Eric Shipton and Jack Longland (of previous Everest expeditions). Over 350 attended, including Trilby Wells, her sister Paddy and brother-in-law John Hirst. The speeches by the "Everesters" and the President were separated by songs from Messrs Hirst and Spilsbury. One of these songs, entitled "Everest 1953", is reproduced in the 1954 F.R.C.C. Journal, sung to the tune of Widdicombe Fair, with a chorus ending "Ed Hillary, Tensing and all". This Dinner was described as "perhaps the outstanding social weekend in the history of the Club- the afterglow of a great adventure which can never be repeated". And two sisters from the tiny Yorkshire hamlet of Denton were there to share in the experience.

Biddy and Trilby, incidentally, had been elected as Honorary Members of the Pinnacle Club earlier in 1953, at the Annual Meeting, along with eight other remaining Original Members- another honour for the sisters. In her interviews later, Trilby spoke about the 1950s, saying that she and the other 'older' members of the club were so impressed by the increase in standards of climbing shown by the newer and younger members of the Pinnacle Club. She particularly mentioned Gwen Moffatt and Nea Morin, but said there were so many others.

At the end of 1953 came a major, but sad, occasion for Trilby Wells as this signalled the end of her time as Head mistress of the Margaret Macmillan School in Bradford. On December 22nd, Miss E. Hardaker (the P.T. Inspector) called at the school with others "to say goodbye to the retiring Head Teacher", as recorded in the School Logbook. The next day was actually Trilby's last day at school and a delegation comprising "the Director of Education, the School Medical Officer and the Chief Woman Inspector came to say 'goodbye' to the retiring Head Teacher". The Logbook continues: "Miss E. Wells retires today from her post as Head Teacher of the School. She was presented with a silver tea-service and tray, and a bowl of bulbs from children past and present, teachers, the school medical officer and the doctor at the Child Guidance Clinic". Trilby remembered that they had tea and sandwiches and cakes after the presentation, though she "didn't like the fuss!"

So into 1954, and now Trilby wells had more time on her hands. She was now approaching 65 and Biddy 59, but both of them were still remarkably fit and healthy, and were active walkers. Trilby continued as President of the Social Guild at St. John's Church, Ben Rhydding and on a couple of evenings arranged entertainment by the Bradford Gilbert and Sullivan Society. She was also still Vice-President of the Pinnacle Club and attended meetings in that capacity during 1954. There was an Easter Pinnacle Club Meet at Coniston though it is not known if any of the Wells sisters were there. Their friend Blanche Eden-Smith (or G as she was known) was still climbing with the Pinnacle Club, and also with Harry Kelly. Kelly was still editor of the Fell and Rock Guide Books to the Lake District, and by 1953 he had edited five of the Third Series of books. He was still to edit another half a dozen guides up to 1959, as well as reprints up to 1966. For this work he received tremendous respect from all in the climbing world, as both an editor and a climber, despite the reservations of some climbers when Kelly refused to include grades above V.S. (Very Severe). Nevertheless, Kelly's contribution to climbing in Britain was much valued. He had been a good friend to the Wells sisters since before 1920.

John Hirst travelled to Skye in 1954, this time without Paddy, to attend the Fell and Rock meet at Sligachan, in a group of thirty-two members, including Bentley Beetham, A.B. Hargreaves and Tony Moulam. The latter had started editing North Wales guide books in 1950 (the Carneddau) and continued to do so for another twenty years.

In the summer of 1954 the Pinnacle Club held an Alpine Meet near Briancon, and in September there was the usual Yorkshire Meet, this time held in Wharfedale and hosted by the Wells sisters, Biddy and Trilby. Climbing standards continued to improve within the club, with ladies leading V.S. climbs on Tremadog, Clogwyn Du'r Arddu, Tryfan and Ogwen cliffs, as well as in the Llanberis Pass area.

A Wells family reunion came at the end of 1954 at the Fell and Rock Annual Dinner, as Paddy and John Hirst sat with Trilby and Biddy to hear tales from the famous Swiss mountaineer and author Andre Roch. Held once again at the Royal Oak, Keswick, speeches were punctuated as usual by some choice excerpts from the repertoire of Messrs. Hirst and Spilsbury. Biddy and Trilby spent the next day walking the Lakeland fells in the rain.

Meanwhile Mabel Barker, mentioned in earlier chapters, was still living at Caldbeck, walking the northern fells and joining in local community events. She welcomed lots of visitors to her home at Friar Row including old friends, climbers, ex-pupils and her family. She was to remain at her cottage at Friar Row until 1961.

So to 1955 and Trilby and Biddy Wells had now moved from their home at Moorland View to a new home at Linden Garth, on Wheatley Lane, Ben Rhydding. Most probably, the old house was too large for just the two of them, and a smaller home made more sense. Biddy was to have ten happy years at this new house. Both of them were still able to attend the Pinnacle Club Annual Dinner meet, which seems to have moved to February (from New Year) on a regular basis. The 1955 Dinner was held at the Pen-y-Gwryd Hotel, from where activities included skiing and mountain walking. This was followed by an Easter meet attended by both sisters at Coniston, which included the A.G.M., at which Mrs. Bryan took over the Presidency, and Trilby ceased to be a Vice President.

Travel to the mountains was now much easier than in the earlier days, and there is an intriguing paragraph in Shirley Angell's book "Pinnacle Club", where she describes vividly, in the 1950s, the women climbers from the London area jumping on a coach on Friday evening, travelling up the A5 to Ogwen and pitching camp about 3.00 or 4.00 a.m. After snatching a couple of hours sleep, and a quick breakfast, they then spent two days on the crags and mountains, before an overnight coach trip back to London, arriving in the capital at about 4.00 a.m. An early train home, shower and food, and off to work on Monday morning! A quite remarkable achievement, and it shows the commitment these women had for climbing and walking regularly.

In her later interviews, Trilby spoke of weekend walks with her sister Biddy on Ilkley Moor, to Upper Wharfedale and in the area of the Three Peaks in Ribblesdale. This was probably because they were now feeling their age, though their interviewer dare not suggest this! Trilby did say they were no longer rock climbing like in their younger days, but they did visit Cwm Dyli and the Lake District on quite a few occasions in the 1950s. Included in these visits was the Fell and Rock Club Dinner at the Royal Oak at the end of 1955, where once again there was the same family reunion as the previous year. Once again they each "signed in" as "Miss E. Wells" and "Miss N. Wells", along with Mr. and Mrs Hirst. Here the chief guests were John Jackson and Charles Evans of the successful Kangchenjunga ascent. John Hirst was joined by Lawson Cook for the usual singing, as Harry Spilsbury was acting as Chairman for the evening. Hirst's song "the Conqueror of Kangchenjunga" was reproduced in the 1956 Fell and Rock Journal.

The Annual Dinner meet of the Pinnacle Club was held at the Old Dungeon Ghyll Hotel in February 1956, where the Wells sisters were fascinated by a slide show given by Monica Jackson, about her expedition to the Himalayas. She and her colleagues from the Ladies Scottish Climbing Club co-authored the excellent book about the expedition, "Tents in the Clouds". The Easter meet of the Pinnacle Club in 1956 was held at Cwm Dyli and again included the Annual Meeting. The three Wells sisters were now some of the oldest members of the club, but still contributed to the general running of the club. Incidentally, in the 1956 F.R.C.C. Journal, Dorothy Pilley-Richards writes of "The Good Young Days" of the Fell and Rock, an excellent article giving an insight into climbing clothing and equipment of the time, the cost of accommodation, and some characters of the 1920s. She goes on to mention certain people who influenced her early climbing career, such as A.W. Wakefield, Eustace Thomas, G.A. Solly, Harry and Pat Kelly, and Blanche Eden-Smith;

after naming several other "greats", she writes of "John Hirst and the Wells sisters". How good it is to see the names of the three sisters from Denton mentioned in such exalted mountaineering company. They were popular in the Fell and Rock as well as the Pinnacle Club. John Hirst's personality is mentioned in F. Lawson Cook's article in the same Journal, as John initiated Lawson Cook into the art of rock climbing and later to the Rucksack Club. Cook states that he was "unable to resist the temptation to join musically…..in one of the after dinner sing-songs organised by him, at which Gilbert and Sullivan items were prominent". Lawson Cook also wrote of his meeting some of the first members of the Pinnacle Club, including the Wells sisters, at Middle Row, Wasdale, in 1921.

Paddy and John Hirst again travelled to Scotland in 1956, while Trilby and Biddy mainly stayed closer to home. Biddy was still teaching at the Margaret Macmillan School in Bradford, with Trilby still devoting a lot of time to Church matters. In March 1956, Trilby was once again at the Bradford Diocesan Conference, and she is again mentioned in newsletters as being involved in many church activities and social events. She was to remain a member of the Diocesan Conference until 1960.

October 27th 1956 was the date for the Fell and Rock Jubilee Dinner, celebrating 50 years since its inception. The three sisters felt it was an occasion not to be missed and duly signed in as "Trilby Wells" and "Biddy Wells" along with "Annie Hirst". Dorothy Pilley-Richards had flown in especially from America; George Abraham was an invited guest; a special cake in the shape of a relief map of the Lake District was cut with an ice axe; and the cover of the menu card was designed by renowned mountain artist W. Heaton Cooper. As usual, songs from John Hirst and partners were prominent after the speeches. On the following morning (Sunday), Trilby and Biddy attended a Fell and Rock Jubilee Thanksgiving Service at St. John's Parish Church in Keswick, though Paddy chose to go out on the hills with her husband! John's song "The Club" is published in the 1957 Journal.

In 1957 Trilby attended the Pinnacle Club Yorkshire Meet at the tiny hamlet of Appletreewick, just north of Bolton Abbey, in Wharfedale. Paddy and John meanwhile embarked on an epic journey to Scotland in May of that year, leaving Preston in a motor coach, picking up thirty people in Kendal, Penrith, Carlisle and Inverness, before finally reaching Ullapool. They climbed Stac Polly and Cul Beag on day one of the Fell and Rock Meet, and then Ben Wyvis the following day. After a day's washout, they joined several others in an ascent of the tops of An Teallach on May 21st. Paddy was praised in the account of the meet (along with other ladies) "for their lavish provision throughout the meet" of tea and food- no mention of her mountaineering achievements! Next day, a sea trip for Paddy to the Summer Isles saw her on the summit of Tanera Mor. Later in the week an ascent was made of Ben More Coigach. In the evenings there were colour slide shows and talks, plus some "very topical and amusing recitations" by Paddy Hirst, (not John!). At the Fell and Rock Dinner in 1957 there are no signatures of any of the Wells sisters, though John Hirst was there to sing his usual song, this one entitled "Blue-print of a President", again reproduced in the 1958 Journal.

1958 seems a blank year for the Wells sisters in terms of mountaineering, as they do not appear to have been on many walking or climbing meets. They did attend the Pinnacle Club A.G.M. at the Easter Meet, however. Trilby again mentioned in her later interviews her great interest (and no doubt her vicarious pleasure) in hearing about the Pinnacle Club members' exploits in these her later years.

"I always took an interest in foreign expeditions carried out by women from the club, throughout the 50s and 60s, and even later when people came to visit me". Pinnacle Cub members were now climbing in Norway, the Alps, Dolomites, Atlas Mountains, North America and the Himalayas.

The 1958 Yorkshire Meet was held at Grassington in the autumn, with good weather enabling both walking and climbing to take place. Biddy and Trilby Wells would be likely to be there, it being only a few miles from their home, but we have no record of their presence on the meet.

At the 1958 Fell and Rock Dinner at the Royal Oak Biddy and Trilby met up with sister Paddy and her husband John. He joined Harry Spilsbury in a song about "the risks of climbing and the benefits of luck and pluck", and then contrasted the hardships of mountain weather with the luxury of hot baths! Bill Tilman was the chief guest and speaker. However, the year was a sad year for many as it signalled the end of an era in mountaineering. On September 6th, 1958, Geoffrey Winthrop Young, climber, author, poet and educationist, sadly passed away.

Geoffrey Winthrop Young was the husband of Eleanor (Len) Slingsby, daughter of the great Cecil Slingsby, from Carleton near Skipton. She was of course a great friend of the Wells sisters and an early member of the Pinnacle Club. Geoffrey had been a great supporter of the idea of an all-female climbing club back in 1920, and he and Harry Kelly, among others, had praised the inauguration of the club in 1921. Geoffrey had worked for the Rockefeller Trust; was an excellent linguist; had been instrumental in the founding of Gordonstoun School and the first Outward Bound Schools; had a dozen seasons in the Alps; ran the Friends' Ambulance Unit at Ypres and in Italy in Word War One when he lost a leg; climbed and walked after the war despite his disability; wrote books and poems; ran the famous Pen-y-Pass parties; became President of the Alpine Club, and was the first President of the British Mountaineering Council. He died at the age of 82. Eleanor was much younger and survived him. He would be sadly missed and he was certainly a very remarkable man!

So to 1959 and Pinnacle Club members were again active in the Alps and Himalayas, as well as in the U.K. Biddy and Trilby walked in the Dales and the Lakes, and in September they were at the traditional Yorkshire meet, which was held at the Hill Inn, Chapel-le Dale, near the foot of Ingleborough. They joined six other members, including Lilian Bray and Marjorie Wood, for a weekend of excellent weather and very long walks. Both sisters again attended the 1959 Fell and Rock Dinner along with sister Paddy and her husband John. Trilby ended the year by being a delegate at the Bradford Diocesan Conference in December.

1960 was another good year for the Wells sisters. Paddy again visited Scotland with husband John, and Biddy and Trilby spent time walking in the Dales. However there is no record of any of the three sisters visiting the hut at Cwm Dyli in 1959 nor in 1960. The two younger sisters now had more time on their hands together as Biddy Wells had decided to retire from her teaching post at the Margaret Macmillan School in 1960. Biddy now began a "friendship" with Middleton Hospital, across the river Wharfe from her Ben Rhydding home, and close to her birthplace of Denton. Every week from immediately after her retirement, Biddy would visit the patients at the hospital, to talk to them, particularly the "old folks", who often had no other visitors. When Biddy Wells died six years later, a seat with an inscribed plaque was placed in the grounds in her memory, donated by her sister Trilby.

In February of 1960 all three Wells sisters were at the Annual Dinner of the Pinnacle Club, where they were joined by their long-time friend Dr. Katie Corbett. Corbett appeared very frail and the sisters felt that this occasion might be the last time they would be together. They were to be proved right, because on June 22nd 1960, Dr. Corbett passed away aged 82. A Founder Member of the Pinnacle Club, she had been a member for thirty-nine years. She had obtained a degree at Manchester University in 1905 and had worked for Lancashire Council's Child Welfare Department for thirty-two years. In World War One she had served in Serbia with a Women's Hospital Unit. After being Treasurer of the Pinnacle Club in 1923, she was elected President from 1929 to 1931. In 1926, Dr Corbett attempted Mont Blanc with Trilby Wells and Sam Hall on the club's first Alpine Meet. She had to stop just below the summit, affected by the altitude, but the other two made it to the summit. A proud achievement for the two ladies and for the Pinnacle Club. Dr. Corbett had a formidable reputation as a fast driver, but also as a super-cool passenger. She had a strong and determined personality, and a gentleness and friendliness to all she met. She was also on the Club's second Alpine Meet, with Trilby Wells, in 1928, and supported Biddy, Trilby and Bray on their successful traverse of the Cuillin Ridge of Skye. Corbett and the Wells sisters had shared many adventures together, and Trilby's school had been evacuated close to Corbett's home in World War Two. Each year, despite her frailty, she was brought by friends to the Annual Dinner and maintained an interest in the club right up to her death. A measure of the esteem in which Dr. Corbett was held is the fact that Lilian Bray, Joan Cochrane and Trilby Wells all wrote about her in the 1959-60 Pinnacle Club Journal.

To end the year, both Trilby and Biddy went to the Fell and Rock Dinner, once again signing in using their nicknames, B. Wells and

T. Wells. John Hirst again sang a song, this time about the President, entitled "Jekyll and Hyde", containing the usual harmless sarcasm and wit found in most of his compositions.

A SLOWING DOWN IN THE 60s

1961 began with a Pinnacle Cub New Year Meet at Cwm Dyli, and then the Annual Dinner at the Pen-y-Gwryd Hotel in Snowdonia on February 17th-19th. Forty members attended the dinner as well as invited guests, and four Founder Members of the Pinnacle Club were present to celebrate forty years of the club: Paddy Hirst, Trilby Wells, Biddy Wells and Lilian Bray. Paddy was now 76 years old, Trilby 71 and Biddy 66, but they were still proud to be "not so active" members of the club, as Trilby later described them. Ken Tarbuck, of the Tarbuck knot fame and a member of the Wayfarers' Club, was the guest speaker, and a slide show followed the dinner. Some members climbed to V.S. standard in Llanberis Pass the next day. The Wells sisters went walking!

At the Easter meet held in Wasdale, the Annual Meeting recorded the sadness felt by all members at the loss of Dr. Corbett. Her ashes were scattered on the slopes of Snowdon, as per her final wishes, on the weekend of the Anniversary Dinner. It was also recorded at the Annual Meeting that a "generous gift" from Biddy and Trilby Wells had paid for major repair bills at the Emily Kelly Hut in Cwm Dyli, particularly the woodworm treatment. Yet another example of the Wells sisters' generosity.

The 1961 Fell and Rock Journal contained an obituary of their friend Dr. Corbett (who had been a long-time member of the F.R.C.C.), which was written by Trilby Wells, and which described her as an excellent fell walker and mountaineer, with some climbing experience. Despite her weak lung, and regular bouts of breathlessness, (hence her stopping before the summit of Mont

Blanc), she was able to participate in many mountaineering exploits, and was renowned for seldom giving up easily.

Apart from losing a dear friend in Corbett, the three Wells sisters suffered an even greater loss in 1961 with the death of their brother Thomas in Bradford on August 16th, aged 73. Once again, the three sisters travelled to the tiny Church of St. Helen at Denton, for the internment. Thomas Wells was buried in the churchyard in the same grave as his parents, Cooper and Jane, and his sister Mary.

On a brighter note, the year saw the publication of "Space Below my Feet" by Gwen Moffatt, to rave reviews from mountaineering publications and journals. An accomplished climber and alpinist, she was at the time the only female professional guide in Britain, and her book is still regarded as a milestone in climbing literature.

Yet another death occurred in 1961, and it was someone who was well-known to Trilby and Biddy. Mabel Barker, who had been visited years before by the Wells sisters, was still living in Caldbeck in the northern Lake District, but in 1961 she had become seriously ill with lung cancer- not surprising as she had been a heavy smoker for many years. In early August she was admitted to hospital, and sadly died on the last day of August, 1961. She would be missed by many of her contemporaries, not least Trilby and Biddy. Mabel's list of first ascents stretched from 1923 to 1937; and her contribution to ideas of "alternative" education, which influenced both Trilby and Biddy Wells, was immeasurable. She had lived life to the full, with a passion for nature and for wild places; she loved the hills and fells where she spent her final years.

In church matters, both Trilby and Biddy were still very active at St. John's Church in Ben Rhydding, and June 6th saw Trilby once again at the Bradford Diocesan Conference, where Dr. Coggan gave his last address as Bishop of Bradford. Trilby reported back to the church council, and she also sat on the Finance committee of the Parish Church Council. It was proposed and seconded that Trilby Wells (and Mr. H. Farrar of Ben Rhydding) be elected as representatives to the Diocesan Council for the next three years. Trilby gladly accepted. There was also a generous gift of several new "kneelers" in the ministers' stalls, once again paid for by the Wells sisters.

So 1962 arrived and the Pinnacle Cub held its Dinner Meet at the Old Dungeon Ghyll Hotel in Langdale at the start of the year, followed by the Annual Meeting at Cwm Dyli over Easter weekend. A further meet was held at Whitsun at the hut. Two Pinnacle Club expeditions took place in 1961 and 1962 to the Himalayas, and again Trilby spoke of her pleasure in hearing about these trips at meetings held later. She welcomed the expansion and variety of the club's climbing exploits over those forty years. Other meets were held at Froggatt and in Wales.

On a family note, John H. Hirst, stepson of Paddy, had become President of the Rucksack Club in 1962, following in his father's footsteps. He was regarded as a fine after-dinner speaker, with humour and knowledge; he was a regular organiser and photographer of club meets; was a physically fit walker and climber; had been to the Alps with his father in 1936; and had completed a solo walking trip in Corsica in 1939. John H. Hirst certainly kept up the family tradition of mountaineering and was to remain a member of the club until his death in 2001.

The 1962 Fell and Rock Dinner took place at the end of the year and surprisingly the list of those attending did not include any of the Wells sisters. This was the first time for many years that this had happened.

The following year saw a Pinnacle Club Dinner in February

followed by an Easter Meet. The Annual Meeting recorded more sad news- the death of Blanche Eden-Smith. "G", as she was known to her friends, had been a prolific climber, completing many routes with Harry Kelly. She had joined the Fell and Rock in 1919 and was a keen all-round sportswoman, playing tennis, cricket and hockey (to county standard), loved horse riding and motor cycling and was a keen swimmer outdoors in lakes and rivers. As a music lover she was also an accomplished violinist. She was very fit on the mountains, whether climbing or walking, and had made the first ascent of Moss Ghyll Grooves with Kelly. Her obituary in the Fell and Rock Journal, written by Harry Kelly, describes her as modest, gracious and kind to all who met her. She was unfortunate in that her health deteriorated in 1961 and 1962 and she had a leg amputated before her death in 1963. "Mrs. Eden-Smith leaves a memory of bright companionship for those who were privileged to become acquainted with her through the medium of the hills" wrote Kelly. In her interviews, Trilby Wells specifically mentioned certain female climbers who had passed away and who were sorely missed. These names included Katie Corbett, Lilian Bray and Blanche Eden-Smith. This year also saw the deaths of two more well-known mountaineers; Bentley Beetham and Graham Macphee, both guidebook writers, and both known to the Wells sisters.

A number of meets were held at Cwm Dyli and a Pinnacle Club group climbed in Chamonix in 1963. Trilby said that in the late 50s and early 60s she and Biddy completed many walks in the Dales and also on Ilkley Moor, but that their climbing days were definitely over! They did, however, meet up with club members whenever they visited Yorkshire, as several did in 1963. Towards the end of that year, there was once again a Wells family reunion at the Annual Fell and Rock Dinner in the Lakes, where the three sisters were joined by

John Hirst. At a nearby table sat two other Ilkley climbers, Jean and Des Birch, who had climbed for several years with Arthur Dolphin, and who were teachers at Ilkley and Otley Grammar schools.

1964 saw a big change in Biddy's health, and Trilby later commented that Biddy felt unwell for the last couple of years of her life. The two sisters still lived together in Ben Rhydding, and only occasionally ventured out for walks in 1964. The church activities were invaluable in their social life, and in 1964 Trilby ceased to be a representative on the Bradford Diocesan Council. Trilby said that she was praised and thanked for her work and commitment to the Diocese in a letter from the Bishop of Bradford. The Pinnacle Club continued to thrive with membership at 126 in 1964, and Trilby and Biddy were able to attend the Annual Dinner in February where Dennis Gray and Tom Patey were guest speakers.

And so to1965 and a special visitor came to the Pinnacle Club Hut at Cwm Dyli- Dawa Tensing of Everest fame. There were also several meets during the year, including a Yorkshire Meet in Swaledale. However, the year was marred by the death of Biddy Wells, the first of our trio of mountaineering sisters to pass away. The local newspaper, The Ilkley Gazette, noted her death as follows:

"WELLS. September 12th 1965, suddenly at Linden Garth, Wheatley Avenue, Ben Rhydding, Sarah Ellen (Nellie), youngest daughter of the late Mr. and Mrs. Cooper Wells and beloved sister of Emily". A service was held at St. John's Church on September 16th, followed by cremation.

This was a devastating blow to Trilby in particular as she had spent virtually her whole life in companionship with Biddy. Noticeable, too, is the fact that there is no mention of sister Paddy in the newspaper, though she and husband John were still alive and living in Lancashire. The 1965-66 Pinnacle Club Journal No. 12 contains an "In Memoriam" to Biddy written by Lilian Bray and Mabel Jeffrey. Bray wrote that she never knew her proper name, "she was just Biddy". She was praised for her leading ability on climbs, for her service to the Pinnacle Club on the Committee and as Secretary; and Bray reminisced about the famous traverse of the Cuillin Ridge, the first by an all-female group. Mabel Jeffrey described Biddy as kind, enthusiastic and fun, and who was an expert leader. By her death the members had lost a true and faithful friend.

Biddy Wells had always been a good leader of climbs with Trilby as her second, yet Trilby had always taken the lead in all other aspects of their lives, Trilby was the Head Teacher and Biddy her Deputy; Trilby was the organiser of social events, Biddy the willing participant. But Trilby now had to make a decision about where to live, and she opted to remaining in her present home at Linden Garth. In fact, Trilby was to spend another seven years at that address.

In the same year as Biddy's death, yet another pioneer of mountaineering died. This was George Abraham, the last of the famous Keswick brothers who had been rock climbers and photographers for many years, and whose early climbs at the beginning of the twentieth century were recorded in some now-famous and highly collectable books.

When mentioning the "In Memoriam" about Biddy by Lilian Bray, this was obviously written immediately after Biddy's death, as the 1965-66 Journal also contains an "In Memoriam" to Lilian Bray herself on the previous page! And it is written by Trilby Wells! In June of 1966, Trilby had attended Bray's ninetieth birthday party, when a special Pinnacle Club Meet and Dinner was held at Church Stretton. Then, in September 1966 there was a special meet in Swaledale, called the "Famous Names" Meet, again attended by Lilian Bray, Mabel Jeffrey, Marjorie Wood, Trilby Wells and several other of the older members. This would be the last time that Trilby met and walked with Lilian Bray, as on November 24th Bray died in her sleep. She had been a Founder Member of the Pinnacle Club and in her seventies was still fit enough to traverse the Snowdon horseshoe. She had been Journal Editor, Committee member and, from 1927-29, President of the Pinnacle Club. Trilby Wells had lost yet another of her friends and fellow members.

The 1966 Fell and Rock Journal also contained an obituary of Biddy Wells, (called Nancy in the text), written by Charles Pilkington. He had first met Biddy and Trilby in 1936 when they were already established mountaineers, and wrote that it seemed natural to say "they" as the two sisters were always together as a pair. He mentioned her traverse of the Cuillin Ridge in 1928, and described her enthusiasm and resolution for climbing. She also "energetically encouraged her amazons to climb and lead". In conclusion, he wrote: "Another pioneer passes but leaves her enthusiasm for others to carry forward".

We do not know the exact date or even year, but it was during this period that Trilby visited the Old Dungeon Ghyll Hotel in Langdale, this time not for a climbing meet, but simply to visit old friends Sid and Jammy Cross. Certainly the 1966 February Dinner was held there, but Trilby spoke of making a special journey with a friend to visit the "O.D.G." Sid and Jammy Cross had been at the hotel since 1949, and were close friends of the members of the Pinnacle Club. Sid was well-known for his services to Mountain Rescue, for which he was to receive an M.B.E., and he was also a keen supporter of the Outward Bound movement and the Duke of Edinburgh Award Scheme. An excellent climber and a guide-book writer, he became President of the Fell and Rock in 1978-80. Trilby spoke so affectionately about Sid and his wife Jammy, and how kind they had been to the Pinnacle Club. Trilby was now in her seventies and only really able to walk locally. Also, her eyesight was beginning to trouble her, but she retained a great interest in everything to do with the Pinnacle Club.

1967 began with a New Year Pinnacle Club Meet at Pen-y-Gwryd, which Trilby apparently was able to attend. Later that year, a ban on walking and climbing occurred in Wales and the Lake District, due to an outbreak of Foot and Mouth Disease, and this limited the activities of many outdoor enthusiasts. However, the ban was lifted early in 1968, in time for the Pinnacle Club Annual Dinner Meet in February at the Old Dungeon Ghyll. Soon after this dinner, Sid and Jammy Cross were to retire from the task of running the hotel, so it was a good opportunity for members to have a final chance to experience their excellent hospitality. The Fell and Rock also held a meeting at the hotel, again an opportunity to pay homage to Sid and Jammy. At the meeting, respects were also paid to Mabel Jeffrey, a friend of Trilby Wells, who had died earlier. She was also a Pinnacle club member, was President for the war years, and had remained active until a year before her death.

There was the usual Pinnacle Club Yorkshire Meet in 1968, led by Alison Adam and Chris Woods. This had somehow developed into an "older members meet", and Trilby Wells was delighted that each year she could meet up with fellow club members and hear all the news about club events and successes.

Trilby journeyed to the Pen-y-Gwryd Hotel in Snowdonia for the 1969 Pinnacle Club Dinner in February, and in the Pinnacle Club Journal no.14, 1969-70, Trilby was asked to write an article called "The Early Days". She began by quoting from one of John Hirst's poems, and was delighted that the club was now nearly fifty years old. Trilby reminisced abut Middle Row in Wasdale; spoke of early members Blanche Eden-Smith and Lilian Bray, and of course Pat Kelly, "our Founder". She again praised the support of "menfolk" in the preamble to, and the setting up of, the Pinnacle Club in 1921, particularly male members of the Rucksack Club. Trilby also lists Almscliff, Stanage and Laddow as examples of "practice meets", with larger meets in Wales and the Lakes. Each "rope" arranged for a sound leader, a good second and a novice or two. She continued: "If you were a novice you carried the rope; if you were a second and your leader cared to change her footwear on a difficult pitch, you carried her boots! I have often carried Bray's boots when she changed to stockinged feet- she always said I was a good second!"

Trilby also wrote about the joy and pleasure obtained by early members in the huts, after a day's climbing or walking. She mentions riding bareback on the fat grey pony in Wasdale; the Gilbert and Sullivan sing-songs to Bray's piano playing; one-act plays written and performed by members; and countless games of charades.

Two other events are highlighted. Trilby writes: "Six of us were the first women to go down Gaping Ghyll, at the invitation of the Yorkshire Ramblers. This was a great adventure in those days….. Of the six I believe I am the only one left", (the group had included Katie Corbett and Biddy Wells), " and of the three of us who were the first all-women's party to traverse the Cuillins from Glen Brittle, I know I am the sole survivor". There is a wonderful photograph of the Gaping Ghyll party alongside the description.

The 1960s had been eventful again for Trilby Wells, though there were many sad occasions as she lost a sister and several close friends. Nevertheless, this article was a fitting way to end the decade and move into the 1970s.

THE FINAL DECADES

The 1970s began with a change of venue for the Pinnacle Club Annual Dinner. New owners had replaced Sid and Jammy Cross at the Old Dungeon Ghyll and they appeared less welcoming to climbers. Club members instead attended the Dinner at the Glenridding Hotel at Ullswater. There is no comment about the quality of the dinner nor the accommodation at the new venue, though they did not return the following year.

Paddy Wells was now aged 86, and she and John were still members of the Rucksack Club and of the Fell and Rock. Paddy also remained faithful to the Pinnacle Club. However, October 1970 brought a sad end to their marriage when John Hirst passed away. John had been a great supporter of the Pinnacle Club, and an excellent poet, song-writer and singer. He had married Paddy Wells in 1922, he being a widower with two young sons. In 1944, he became President of the Rucksack Club, and was made an Honorary Member in 1955. He remained active all his life, and had completed the Munros in Scotland in 1947 with wife Paddy. In his seventies he climbed Longland's Climb on Clogwyn Du'r Arddu, and continued to walk up Lake District mountains until shortly before his death. His songs contained wit and kind ridicule, never unkind nor hurtful, but usually very funny. The songs were often based on Gilbert and Sullivan tunes. His great friend was Harry Spilsbury, who often accompanied him at club sing-songs and dinners. In 1922, John Hirst had published "Songs of the Mountaineers", a collection of mountaineering songs familiar to climbers all over the U.K. He was very well respected in the Rucksack Club, and in his obituary,

Fred Piggott wrote that "no-one did more during his long years of membership to sustain the happiness and well-being of the Club". Paddy was to live for another three years after John's death. John Hirst had played an integral part in the lives of the three Wells sisters from Denton.

1971 was to be a very special year for the Pinnacle Club as it celebrated its fifty years anniversary. The Annual Dinner, which was bound to be a bit special, was held at the Pen-y-Gwryd Hotel, the same venue as the first official meeting way back in 1921. There were special guests in Don and Audrey Whillans and H.M. Kelly, a festive menu, and gold-printed menu cards illustrated in beautiful water colours by member Marjorie Wood. To cap it all, there were three of the Original Members of the Pinnacle Club from 1921 present at the Dinner. All three were Yorkshire ladies and all three from the local area: Eleanor Winthrop Young (originally from Carleton, near Skipton); Paddy Hirst (nee Wells) and Trilby Wells (both from Denton near Ilkley). Trilby commented on this dinner as being a very special day in her memory. She was so delighted that "we'd lasted fifty years", and lamented the fact that sister Biddy, friends Corbett and Bray, and others, were not around to celebrate this great milestone. In all, eighty people attended a momentous dinner, held in two rooms because of the large numbers. Evelyn Leech, (nee Lowe), who had joined the club in 1929, proposed a toast to the special guests, despite her serious ill-health. Many felt this would be her last club dinner, and so it turned out to be. She was yet another great friend of the Wells sisters and had been Hut Secretary and Club President from 1946 to 1948. Nea Morin wrote an appreciation of her life for the 1973 Journal and several members visited Anglesey on October 3rd for Evelyn's memorial service. To all who knew her she was a very special person.

The following year saw Trilby Wells move away from the home she had shared with Biddy at Linden Garth, after being on her own for nearly seven years. Trilby decided to move into a home for the elderly (she was 83 that year), and chose a home in Wells Road, Ilkley, before later moving to Ghyll Court in 1979. Once again, Trilby's eyesight was worsening, and she began to struggle with reading and with her writing. This was unfortunate as she said she had always been a keen letter writer all her life. She was still quite active though in terms of walking, and was determined not to become housebound. She still enjoyed some local, short walks and was able to continue this for a few more years.

The Pinnacle Club Annual Dinner of 1972 was held at the Skiddaw Hotel in Keswick, which Trilby managed to attend. This was probably because the club had invited Sid and Jammy Cross as guests so that they could formally thank them for their help and hospitality in the past. Trilby would not wish to miss the occasion, as the couple were her close friends. They frequently wrote to Trilby for several years after their retirement when Trilby became less mobile and was unable to attend dinners and meets.

The church at Ben Rhydding was still important to Trilby at this late stage of her life, and she attended church services as often as she could. She also went to local musical concerts at every opportunity, and had joined the local Ilkley Townswomen's Guild. Her social life had not stagnated, even if her climbing days had ceased.

Sadness came in 1973, however, as Trilby lost the last of her sisters. It had not been an eventful year for Trilby until November, when sadly, Paddy Hirst passed away, at the grand age of 89. The 1974-76 Pinnacle Club Journal contained just one line under the heading "Deaths", simply stating "Mrs. John Hirst (original member) November 1973". This was really surprising as Paddy had been a pioneer rock climber before 1920, a Founder Member of the Pinnacle Club and had continued her membership right up to her death. However, the club made amends in the next Journal, No 17 (1977-80) when Len Winthrop Young wrote an excellent obituary listing Paddy's qualities and achievements. She described Paddy (or Annie) as, "the eldest of the three famous Wells sisters, all extremely good climbers and outstanding personalities… I personally regret that I did not meet them until 1920… though I only lived on the other side of Ilkley Moor". Paddy became the second President of the Pinnacle Club (after Len) and also held the posts of Secretary and Librarian. She climbed with husband John Hirst (whom she married in 1922) in the Alps and the Dolomites, and also completed the Munros in Scotland, Paddy being the first woman to do so. Len Winthrop Young mentioned their last meeting at the 1971 Anniversary Dinner of the Pinnacle Club, and concludes:" Paddy is remembered, always in association with her sisters, as a first-rate climber, shining with vital friendliness and the best of Yorkshire sincerity!" A kind tribute to the oldest of the Wells sisters from Denton.

So now only Trilby remained of those three Denton sisters, and indeed of the whole Wells family. She was also aware that many of her contemporaries were ageing and many had already passed away. She continued with her local walks, attending church on Sundays and going to local social events in Ilkley. She received visitors at her Ilkley home and loved to receive news of the Pinnacle Club events, meets and dinners. She took a kind of vicarious pleasure in hearing of the exploits of the current club members, and commented in her later interviews on how "technical" (her word) modern climbing had become compared to a much more simple and unsophisticated activity she had engaged in during the 1920s and 30s. She was nevertheless truly impressed by modern women's climbing and mountaineering.

The rest of the 1970s was as eventful as ever for the Pinnacle Club, with members climbing all over the world, and continuing to hold meets and dinners in various parts of the U.K. One notable event was the 1978 Annual Dinner at the Wasdale Head Hotel, with Lake District Warden John Wyatt as a guest speaker. Also at that dinner, another guest speaker, Charles Pilkington (who incidentally had written Biddy's obituary for the Fell and Rock Journal), thanked the Pinnacle Club for many happy memories, and then said that it was Trilby Wells who had actually taught him to climb many years before.

In 1979 the death was announced of a member of the Fell and Rock Club named Miss Maisie Greig. This was of note because it was the same Maisie Greig that Trilby Wells had led up a climb in 1925, thus enabling Trilby to change her membership status from an Associate Member to a Full member of the Pinnacle Club. How good that someone who had undertaken their first climb with Trilby Wells had joined the Fell and Rock and had remained a member for fifty years.

One of the Pinnacle Club Journals of the late 1970s contained an interesting article written by Harry Kelly, describing how he and his wife Pat had met "Miss Wells" (later Mrs. Paddy Hirst) at Stool End in the Lake District at Easter 1916. Entitled "Founding days", Kelly wrote about events before and during the establishing of the Pinnacle Club, including the 'mock Inaugural Meeting' which Kelly chaired and which was critically analysed by J. H. Doughty. The men stood down before the genuine (all female) Inaugural Meeting in 1921.

Trilby was still receiving copies of the Journal by post or brought by visitors, and no doubt would have been pleased to read Kelly's comments on the early days. In fact, in a letter in Pinnacle Club archives written by Trilby Wells in February 1980, she writes to thank Sheila Cormack, the Club President, for writing to tell her all about the Club Annual Dinner. Trilby writes:" Although I cannot come to the meets I am still very interested in all the 'doings' of the Club….the only thing that troubles me is my poor eyesight…. I get out for a walk each day when fine". She then asks about plans for the Club's Diamond Anniversary in 1981 and also mentions her "very old friend" Sid Cross. He had written to her before Christmas enclosing the menu card for the Fell and Rock Dinner and an account of the proceedings.

In March of 1980 Trilby also wrote to Shirley Angell who was preparing her history of the Pinnacle Club. In her letter (again in the Club Archives), Trilby tells Shirley Angell about Emily (Pat) Kelly's fatal accident, and how Trilby had later found the missing shoe. It would appear that Shirley Angell must have sent Trilby Wells a draft of her account, and Trilby was replying to set the record straight. Trilby had earlier told Shirley how the missing shoe had been found and buried, and no-one told Harry Kelly in case it should upset him. Once again, Trilby's spidery handwriting shows how her eyesight was weakening, yet her mind was still very alert. Trilby was still able to watch her television and her favourite time was Wimbledon fortnight- a throwback to her youth when she and Biddy had regularly played tennis together.

In 1980, the year of my first interview with her, Trilby Wells appeared on the local radio. John Anscombe presented a programme on Radio Leeds called "Meet the Folks", and this particular programme celebrated the seventy fifth anniversary of the Church of St. John at Ben Rhydding. There were festivals and a thanksgiving service, and John Anscombe wanted to meet and interview local people, particularly those with an interesting tale to tell, and also who might be connected to the church. Who better to talk to than

Miss Emily (Trilby) Wells, who had been connected to the church for 74 of those 75 years? Trilby was duly interviewed, saying she had been present at the institution of every vicar of St. John's up to 1980, but was now having to miss her regular church attendance owing to ill-health. This is the first time she had mentioned her health publicly and when I met her later that year she was very bright and alert and spoke quite eloquently. Trilby spoke on the radio about her roles as Sunday School student and teacher, a Church Council member and (particularly proudly) as a representative of the church on the Bradford Diocesan Council. Later, Trilby spoke about her early days in Ben Rhydding, at the local school where she began her teaching career, and of her time at "the Bradford School" (Margaret Macmillan). This she described as a school for "E.S.N. children" (a term certainly not used today), where she had spent "most of my life". She also said that there were very few of these schools in the country and only one in Bradford. Typically she did not mention how pioneering her work with the curriculum and with the children had been, and how she had extended her influence into other schools in Bradford and into the families of many of her pupils.

Next on the radio came Trilby's sporting background, with happy memories of hockey matches. She claimed that she and her sister had started the hockey club at Ben Rhydding (see earlier chapter) in 1921 which was women-only at first, then mixed, and then "men on their own". They played at the same venue as the present Ben Rhydding Hockey Club, and Trilby said that she played "right inside, then right half, then right back!"

Trilby's climbing career was mentioned, and she described how there were three sisters, the eldest Annie starting first. Harry and Pat Kelly are mentioned, and Trilby spoke of joining the Pinnacle Club and having climbing sessions at Almscliff Crag. She also spoke of the French and Italian Alps, and of course her famous all-women Skye Ridge traverse. Finally, Trilby's love of Gilbert and Sullivan is mentioned, and when asked to choose a piece of music to end the interview, she chose a piece called "Take a pair of sparkling eyes".

This broadcast was a fascinating piece of radio to listen to, and gave further impetus to this author to delve much deeper into Trilby's life. This led to much more detail about her sisters too, and a series of short interviews followed. John Anscombe later confided to a friend that he could probably have done a series of programmes just on Trilby and her sisters!

The initial purpose of my interviewing Trilby Wells was to explore her mountaineering achievements, but what emerged was the multi-faceted life of three sisters, not just one climber. The last interview the author was to have with Trilby Wells was at the end of 1984, though a local climber, Mike Gibbons, did a recorded interview with her in 1985.

The Pinnacle Club Journal of 1979-81 also contained an obituary, that of H. M. (Harry) Kelly, written by Sid Cross; and he also wrote a similar obituary in the 1981 Fell and Rock Journal. How coincidental that in her Radio Leeds programme of 1980 Trilby should speak so highly of Harry Kelly and that he should die that very year. He had of course been an integral part of the Wells sisters' life story, and a good friend, particularly to Paddy. He had also regularly kept in touch with Trilby in her last few years. He had also stayed at Ben Rhydding with Biddy and Trilby. Both obituaries describe him as a forthright personality, with a stubborn nature and at times a difficult person to get to know. But he was also kind and generous, and even gentle in nature, to those who really did get to know him. His climbing exploits are numerous and legendary and his climbing diaries are a very interesting read. He was also a renowned guide-book writer and editor. His last climbs were in 1960 in Langdale. Both obituaries are an excellent read and worthy of this great climbing pioneer.

In 1981 Trilby was still at her home in Ilkley, not being able to travel to the Annual Dinner of the Pinnacle Club at the end of January, held at the Royal Goat Hotel in Beddgelert. This was the sixtieth anniversary of the founding of the Pinnacle Club, and Len Winthrop Young was the sole representative of the remaining Original Members.

The author again visited Trilby to continue researching her life and the lives of her sisters, and though at times somewhat frail and with failing eyesight, her mind was still very alert, and she often had a twinkle in her eye when recalling certain events. She did need prompting at times, and remained quite modest about her many achievements. She showed me the latest Pinnacle Club Journal of March 1981 and wrote a letter (again in the Club archives) to Angela Soper, saying she was "delighted to get the P.C. Journal which you sent", adding that it "has been much enjoyed by some of the folks here". She was now living at Ghyll Court in Ilkley. In the above Journal, Alison Adams writes about the early days of the Pinnacle Club, from 1930 to 1940. She mentions climbing at Almscliff Crag and Embsay, as well as walking in the Yorkshire Dales and the Three Peaks area- all activities in which Trilby and Biddy Wells took part, and which thrilled Trilby to read about after all those years.

The 1982 Annual Dinner was held at the Glenridding Hotel, Ullswater, but again Trilby was unable to attend. The Club also celebrated the fiftieth anniversary of the opening of the Emily Kelly Hut at Cwm Dyli, in November, with invited guests from several kindred clubs, and a huge bonfire and fireworks. There were further short interviews with Trilby in 1982, and I happened to mention that I had soloed the Cuillin Ridge on Skye a few years before. Trilby immediately began to reminisce about her traverse of the ridge and said that they "bivvied somewhere, but didn't sleep very well". When prompted that she and her companions were the first all-female party to complete the traverse she said: "Yes, but we didn't blow our own trumpets!" This was a phrase that Trilby Wells used time and again when talking about her exploits on the mountains and in other walks of life. She remained completely modest to the end of her days. She really loved Glen Brittle after the war, saying she had been back to Skye in the 1950s.

Her other fond memory was the Mont Blanc area; not just the actual mountain, but "the vastness, the scenery, the people". She added: "We climbed Mont Blanc. It was hard but it was enjoyable". She needed prompting about her mountaineering in North Wales, spoke fondly of Tryfan, but could not remember the other big cliff she climbed on. I suggested Lliwedd and she beamed, and agreed that it was a great place to climb, "very good atmosphere, and not far from the hut". Her other great love was the Yorkshire Dales, including Malham and Upper Wharfedale, where there were often mixed groups, "but mostly only women climbers on Pinnacle Club meets!" she emphasised. She was asked about her feelings when elected President of the Pinnacle Club, and she replied it was "a great honour". Again, she was reluctant to boast about her period in office.

In my final interview with Trilby Wells in 1984, I again referred to Pat Kelly's death on Tryfan. "Tragic. I was there you know, on the mountain" she said, but would not discuss the incident any further. It seemed obvious that it had remained in her memory, but that it was a very sad event to recall.

Apart from her radio broadcast, one of the local newspapers, the "Airedale and Wharfedale Observer", published an article about Trilby Wells in 1983. In the article called "Where are they now?" and subtitled "The Singer who scaled Mountains", Trilby's eventful life was documented, including references to her teaching career, her involvement in local amateur operatics and of course her mountaineering career. Trilby recalled the ascent of Mont Blanc: "We had to stay overnight in a wretched hut" before the ascent, and were roped up and wearing crampons. "It was well worth the effort and I have treasured that occasion all my life".

In 1984, the author moved to the Lake District to work for three years, so notes on the Wells sisters were put on the back burner. In early 1985, a local climber, Mike Gibbons of Draughton, near Skipton, was researching the life of Cecil Slingsby, and he interviewed Trilby Wells. She was by now 95 years old and in the taped interview she again talked about Pat Kelly's death on Tryfan. She was still able to speak quite clearly and had a good memory. Asked about Len Winthrop Young, she said she did not know Len's father, Cecil Slingsby, at all but had heard so much about him. She was asked if Eleanor was about the same age as Trilby, and she indignantly replied that Eleanor "is not as old as I am!" Trilby said her mountaineering was mainly in the 1920s and 30s, and that there were three sisters, but "I'm the only one left". She added that climbers today use more equipment than they did back then, and it seemed too mechanised these days.

Later, she again spoke of Geoffrey Winthrop Young, and the day that everyone gathered on the top of Great Gable to commemorate the fallen during the war. She described it as "a horrible day" and once more described how she had helped the parson put on his surplice in the wind and rain. When asked about nostalgia, Trilby said she was "content with what I achieved". What was her most memorable achievement? "Mont Blanc" she replied, "but it was just climbing in snow…More interesting was the Yorkshire Three Peaks!"

As far as is known, this was the last interview Trilby Wells gave, as sadly she died later that year. The Ilkley Gazette of 26th July 1985 carried the news as follows:

"WELLS. July 23rd. Emily (Trilby) aged 96 years peacefully at Ghyll Court, Ilkley, and late of Wheatley Avenue, Ilkley. Service took place at St. John's Church, Ben Rhydding, today Friday July 26th".

On August 2nd 1985 there appeared a short obituary of Trilby in the Ilkley Gazette, though some of the detail is a little wayward to say the least:-

"A retired Ilkley head mistress who had a reputation of being a formidable climber, having climbed Mont Blanc (14,807 ft), the highest summit in W. Europe, has died at the age of 96.

Miss Emily Wells, of Ghyll Court, was born and educated in Denton. After leaving school at 18, she began teaching mentally handicapped children at the Macmillan school in Bradford where she taught until 1953, when she retired.

Miss Wells had always lived in the Ilkley district and was a member of the Townswomen's Guild. She used to be a keen walker and climber and in 1926 received a certificate for climbing Mont Blanc in Switzerland. She also climbed in the Lake District, Italy and the Isle of Skye, when she was a member of two rock climbing clubs, Women's Pina Club and Fellen Rock Club. She also used to play tennis and hockey at Ben Rhydding Sports Club. She moved from her previous home at Crescent House in Wells Road, Ilkley, to Ghyll Court six years ago".

As previously stated, some details are a little strange, especially as the writer of the obituary obviously knew nothing about climbing clubs and their names!

The Reverend Michael Savage, Vicar of St. John's at Ben Rhydding, took the service on July 26th, and funeral arrangements were made by Andrew Wade (Solicitors) of Ilkley. The body was taken by Eaton's undertakers for cremation at Skipton Crematorium; the ashes were collected but it is not known by whom. Many people attended the service, including members of the Pinnacle Club and other mountaineering clubs.

An obituary appeared in the Pinnacle Club Journal No. 20, 1985-87, written by Alison Adams, stating that two names seemed to symbolize the Pinnacle Club to her- "Biddy and Trilby", always said in that order. This was a reference to Biddy always leading on climbs, Trilby always the second. However, the roles were reversed as soon as they reached the ground! Alison spoke of Trilby's character and referred to the sisters as having excellent and humorous acting ability.

Denise Wilson, of nearby Addingham and an ex-President of the Pinnacle Club, also wrote about Trilby in that same Journal, saying she first met Trilby in 1972. She wrote of visiting Trilby in Ilkley on several occasions, and that Trilby was always anxious to hear news of the latest Pinnacle Club ventures. Apparently, when the Journal was read to her, she would always pass comment on the obituaries! Denise Wilson ends by writing: "I feel privileged to have known her".

Thus the end of the story had come for the three Wells sisters from the tiny hamlet of Denton, near Ilkley. Who would have thought that three young women from the Wells family should live through two World Wars, have very successful teaching careers, travel all over the U.K. and Europe, become founders of the first all-women mountaineering club, and undertake so many exciting, adventurous and often pioneering climbing excursions.

Those who knew Trilby Wells in her last years were rewarded by her enthusiasm for life, her wonderful memory and stories, and held an admiration for a remarkable lady.

POSTSCRIPT

Although the story of the Wells sisters effectively ends in 1985 with the death of Trilby, other people closely associated with the sisters lived on. Dorothy Pilley Richards, who had been in the Alps with Paddy in 1921, and who had gone on to climb all over the world, died the following year, 1986. At the age of 92, she had spent New Year at the Glen Brittle memorial Hut on Skye with her nephew and several fellow climbers, and had also been to the Napes Needle Centenary in June of that year. Another climbing great had passed away.

Sid Cross, a long-time friend of all three Wells sisters, particularly Trilby, lived on until the age of 85, dying only in 1998. He was a talented rock climber and contributed so much to mountaineering in general and to Mountain Rescue in particular.

Finally, in 2001, came the death of Paddy Hirst's stepson, John H. Hirst, on the 1st of October, at the age of 87. He had followed in his father's footsteps by becoming President of the Rucksack Club, and again was an experienced mountaineer.

Yet others live on, and perhaps the present members of the Pinnacle Club will write about the next 50 or so years of the Club, remembering always those Founder Members of 1921.

BIBLIOGRAPHY

Presumptuous Pinnacle Ladies. Pinnacle Club 2009. Millrace.

Pinnacle Club. Shirley Angell 1988. Pinnacle Club.

Women Climbing. Birkett and Peascod 1989. A.C. Black.

Women on the Rope. Cicely Williams 1973. Allen & Unwin.

Climbing Days. Dorothy Pilley 1989. Hogarth Press.

A Woman's Reach. Nea Morin 1969. Eyre & Spottiswoode.

Swiss Notes By Five Ladies. Peter A. Marshall & Private Pub. Jean K. Brown 2003.

And Nobody Woke Up Dead. Jan Levi 2006. The Ernest Press.

Pinnacle Club Journals.

Fell and Rock Club Journals.

Rucksack Club Journals.

ABOUT THE AUTHOR

Dennis Wynne-Jones qualified from the University of Wales as a teacher of Physical Education and Geography before gaining a distinction in Outdoor Education at the University of Lancaster.

He taught for twenty-five years in Wharfedale and also spent ten years working in North Wales with pupils with autistic and challenging behaviours. He also ran two Outdoor Education Centres in South Wales and in the Lake District.

Dennis has lectured at National Conferences on 'Leadership in the Outdoors', and on 'Safety in Outdoor Education', whilst publishing articles in The Journal of Adventure Education and Climber and Rambler magazine. He has also authored papers on 'The Effects of Circadian Rhythms on Performance in Outdoor Activities' and 'The Psychology of Solitude in Adventure Education'. In contrast, he has also written articles for the magazine 'Welsh Football'!

In his younger days, Dennis was selected to represent Wales at Football, played Rugby Union for Otley, was an experienced Fell Runner and a WhiteWater Canoeist. He has been a mountaineer for over fifty years, climbing and walking in all seasons throughout the UK and has experience in the Alps, Norway and the Pyrenees. He has also travelled in the mountains of North America, North Africa and the Himalayas.

Now retired, Dennis' hobbies are mountain walking, crown green bowls, and researching mountaineering history and literature.

Lightning Source UK Ltd.
Milton Keynes UK
UKOW07f0404010416

271303UK00009B/20/P